M000230142

Scrum — A Pocket Guide

## Other publications by Van Haren Publishing

Van Haren Publishing (VHP) specializes in titles on Best Practices, methods and standards within four domains:

- IT and IT Management
- Architecture (Enterprise and IT)
- Business Management and
- Project Management

Van Haren Publishing offers a wide collection of whitepapers, templates, free e-books, trainer materials etc. in the **Van Haren Publishing Knowledge Base**: www.vanharen.net for more details.

Van Haren Publishing is also publishing on behalf of leading organizations and companies: ASLBiSL Foundation, CA, Centre Henri Tudor, Gaming Works, IACCM, IAOP, IPMA-NL, ITSqc, NAF, Ngi, PMI-NL, PON, The Open Group, The SOX Institute.

Topics are (per domain):

| IT and IT Management | Architecture (Enterprise and IT) | Project, Program and Risk Management |
|---|---|---|
| ABC of ICT | ArchiMate® | A4-Projectmanagement |
| ASL® | GEA® | ICB / NCB |
| CATS CM® | Novius Architectuur Methode | ISO 21500 |
| CMMI® | TOGAF® | MINCE® |
| CoBIT | | M_o_R® |
| e-CF | **Business Management** | MSP™ |
| Frameworx | BiSL® | P3O® |
| ISO 17799 | EFQM | PMBOK® Guide |
| ISO 27001/27002 | eSCM | PRINCE2® |
| ISO 27002 | IACCM | |
| ISO/IEC 20000 | ISA-95 | |
| ISPL | ISO 9000/9001 | |
| IT Service CMM | OPBOK | |
| ITIL® | SAP | |
| MOF | SixSigma | |
| MSF | SOX | |
| SABSA | SqEME® | |

For the latest information on VHP publications, visit our website: www.vanharen.net.

# Scrum

## A Pocket Guide

Gunther Verheyen

Van Haren
PUBLISHING

# Colophon

| | |
|---|---|
| Title: | Scrum – A Pocket Guide |
| Subtitle: | A smart travel companion |
| Series: | Best Practice |
| Author: | Gunther Verheyen |
| Reviewers: | Ken Schwaber (Scrum co-creator, Scrum.org) |
| | David Starr (Agile Craftsman, Microsoft) |
| | Ralph Jocham (Agile Professional, effective agile) |
| | Patricia Kong (Director of Partners, Scrum.org) |
| | |
| Text editor: | Steve Newton |
| Publisher: | Van Haren Publishing, Zaltbommel, www.vanharen.net |
| ISBN hard copy: | 978 90 8753 720 3 |
| ISBN eBook: | 978 90 8753 794 4 |
| Edition: | First edition, first impression, October 2013 |
| | First edition, second impression, January 2014 |
| | |
| Layout and typesetting: | CO2 Premedia, Amersfoort – NL |
| Copyright: | © Van Haren Publishing, 2013 |

For any further enquiries about Van Haren Publishing, please send an e-mail to: info@vanharen.net

# Foreword by Ken Schwaber

**An outstanding accomplishment that simmers with intelligence.**

*Scrum – A Pocket Guide* is an extraordinarily competent book. Gunther has described everything about Scrum in well-formed, clearly written descriptions that flow with insight, understanding, and perception. Yet, you are never struck by these attributes. You simply benefit from them, later thinking, "That was really, really helpful. I found what I needed to know, readily understood what I wanted, and wasn't bothered by irrelevancies."

I have struggled to write this foreword. I feel the foreword should be as well-written as the book it describes. In this case, that is hard. Read Gunther's book. Read it in part, or read it in whole. You will be satisfied.

Scrum is simple, but complete and competent in addressing complex problems. Gunther's pocket guide is complete and competent in addressing understanding a simple framework for addressing complex problems, Scrum.

**Ken, August 2013**

# Preface

The use of Agile methods continues to grow traction and Scrum is the most widely adopted method for Agile software development. The general level of interest in Scrum is therefore considerable.

Transforming an organization's development approach to Scrum represents quite a challenge. Scrum is not a cookbook 'process' with detailed and exhaustive prescriptions for every imaginable situation. Scrum is a *framework* of principles, roles and rules that thrive on the *people* doing Scrum. The true potential of Scrum lies in the discovery and *emergence* of practices, tools and techniques and in optimizing them for each organization's specific context. Scrum is very much about behavior, much more than it is about process.

The benefits an organization realizes with Scrum depend on the will to remove barriers, think across boxes and embark on a journey of discovery.

The journey starts by playing Scrum. This requires knowledge of the rules of Scrum. This book describes these. This book shows how Scrum implements the Agile mindset, what the rules of the game of Scrum are, and how these rules leave room for a variety of tactics to play the game. The introduction of all essentials of Scrum and the most common tactics for Scrum makes this book a worthwhile read for people, teams, managers and change agents, whether they are already doing Scrum or want to embark on the journey of Scrum.

Ten years ago I started my journey, my path of Agility via Scrum. It has inevitably been a cobblestone path. On my journey I have used Scrum with plenty of teams, in various projects, and at different organizations. I have worked with both large and small enterprises and have coached teams as well as executive management. I was in the fortunate position of then moving to Scrum.org. It's where I shepherd the 'Professional' series of Scrum trainings, courseware and assessments.

I thank Ken Schwaber, David Starr, Ralph Jocham, and Patricia Kong for reviewing early versions of this book and improving it with much appreciated feedback.

I thank all at Van Haren Publishing for their trust and confidence, and for giving me the chance to express my views on Scrum with this book.

I thank my colleagues at Scrum.org for our daily collaboration, the positive action and the energy, and especially Ken Schwaber for our exquisite partnership.

Enjoy reading, and... keep Scrumming.

**Gunther, June 2013**

# Reviews

This Scrum Pocket Guide is outstanding. It is well organized, well written, and the content is excellent. This should be the de facto standard handout for all looking for a complete, yet clear overview of Scrum.

*(Ken Schwaber, Scrum co-creator, Scrum.org)*

Gunther has expertly packaged the right no-nonsense guidance for teams seeking agility, without a drop of hyperbole. This is the book about agility with Scrum I wish I had written.

*(David Starr, Agile Craftsman, Microsoft)*

During my many Scrum training activities I often get asked: "For Scrum, what is the one book to read?" In the past the answer wasn't straight forward, but now it is! The Scrum Pocket Guide is the one book to read when starting with Scrum. It is a concise, yet complete and passionate reference about Scrum.

*(Ralph Jocham, Agile Professional, effective agile.)*

'The house of Scrum is a warm house. It's a house where people are WELCOME.' Gunther's passion for Scrum and its players is evident in his work and in each chapter of this book. He explains the Agile paradigm, lays out the Scrum framework and then discusses the 'future state of Scrum.' Intimately, in about 100 pages.

*(Patricia M. Kong, Director of Partners, Scrum.org)*

# Contents

**1 THE AGILE PARADIGM** .................................................... **13**

| | | |
|---|---|---|
| 1.1 | To shift or not to shift | 13 |
| 1.2 | The origins of Agile | 18 |
| 1.3 | Definition of Agile | 19 |
| 1.4 | The iterative-incremental continuum | 22 |
| 1.5 | Agility can't be planned | 26 |
| 1.6 | Combining Agile and Lean | 28 |

**2 SCRUM** ................................................................ **37**

| | | |
|---|---|---|
| 2.1 | The house of Scrum | 37 |
| 2.2 | Scrum, what's in a name? | 38 |
| 2.3 | Is that a gorilla I see over there? | 41 |
| 2.4 | Framework, not methodology | 44 |
| 2.5 | Playing the game | 46 |
| 2.6 | Core principles of Scrum | 61 |
| 2.7 | The Scrum values | 71 |

**3 TACTICS FOR A PURPOSE** ................................................ **77**

| | | |
|---|---|---|
| 3.1 | Visualizing progress | 78 |
| 3.2 | The Daily Scrum questions | 79 |
| 3.3 | Product Backlog refinement | 80 |

3.4     User Stories ........................................ 81
3.5     Planning Poker ..................................... 83
3.6     Sprint length ...................................... 83
3.7     Scaling Scrum ...................................... 85

**4    THE FUTURE STATE OF SCRUM** ......................... **91**

4.1     Yes, we do Scrum. And... ........................... 91
4.2     The power of the possible product .................. 93
4.3     The upstream adoption of Scrum ..................... 95


Annex A: Scrum vocabulary ............................. 101
Annex B: References ................................... 105
About the author ...................................... 109

# 1 The Agile paradigm

## ■ 1.1  TO SHIFT OR NOT TO SHIFT

The software industry was for a long time dominated by a paradigm of
*industrial* views and beliefs (figure 1.1). This was in fact a copy-paste
of old manufacturing routines and theories. An essential element in
this landscape of knowledge, views and practices was the Taylorist[1]
conviction that 'workers' can't be trusted to undertake intelligent and
creative work. They are expected to only carry out executable tasks.
Therefore their work must be prepared, designed and planned by
more senior staff. Furthermore, hierarchical supervisors must still
vigilantly oversee the execution of these carefully prepared tasks.

Methodology
Plan
Resource management utilization
Project Manager
Direct
Tasks
Control
Money rewards

Figure 1.1  The industrial paradigm

Quality is assured by admitting the good and rejecting the bad batches of outputs. Monetary rewards are used to stimulate desired behavior. Unwanted behavior is punished. It's like carrots and sticks.

The serious flaws of this paradigm in software development are known and well documented. In particular, the Chaos reports of the Standish Group have over and over again revealed the low success rates of traditional software development. The latest of these reports is dated 2011 (Standish, 2011). Many shortcomings and errors resulting from the application of the industrial paradigm in software development are well beyond reasonable levels of tolerance. The unfortunate response seems to have been to lower the expectations. It was accepted that only 10-20% of software projects would be successful. Success in the industrial paradigm is made up of the combination of on time, within budget and including all scope. *Although these criteria for success can be disputed, it is the paradigm's promise.* It became accepted that quality is low, and that over 50% of features of traditionally delivered software applications are never used (Standish, 2002).

Although it is not widely and consciously admitted, the industrial paradigm did put the software industry in a serious crisis. Many tried to overcome this crisis by fortifying the industrial approach. More plans were created, more phases scheduled, more designs made, more work was done upfront, hoping for the actual work to be undertaken to be executed more effectively. The exhaustiveness of the upfront work was increased. The core idea remained that the 'workers' needed to be directed with even more detailed instructions. Supervision was increased and intensified.

And still, little improved. Many flaws, defects and low quality had to be tolerated.

It took some time, but inevitably new ideas and insights started forming following the observation of the significant anomalies of the industrial paradigm. The seeds of a new world view were already sown in the 1990's. But it was in 2001 that these resulted in the formal naming of 'Agile', a turning-point in the history of software development. A new paradigm for the software industry was born (figure 1.2); a paradigm that thrives upon heuristics and creativity, and restoring the respect for the creative nature of the work and the intelligence of the 'workers' in software development.

Figure 1.2 The Agile paradigm

The software industry has good reasons to move fast to the new paradigm; the existing flaws are significant, widely known and the presence of software in society grows exponentially, making it a critical aspect of our modern world. However, by definition, a shift to a new paradigm takes time. And the old paradigm seems to have deep roots. An industrial approach to software development even continues to be taught and promoted as the most appropriate one.

Many say that Agile is too radical and they, therefore, propagate a gradual introduction of Agile practices into the existing, traditional process. However, there is reason to be very skeptical about a gradual evolution, a slow progression from the old to the new paradigm, from waterfall to Agile.

The chances are quite high that a gradual evolution will never go beyond the surface, will not do more than just scratch that surface. New names will be installed, new terms and new practices will be imposed, but the fundamental thinking and behavior of people and organizations will remain the same. Essential flaws will remain untouched; especially the disrespect for people that will lead to the continued treatment of creative, intelligent people as mindless 'workers'.

The preservation of the traditional foundation will keep existing data, metrics and standards in place, and the new paradigm will be measured against these old standards. Different paradigms by their nature consist of fundamentally different concepts and ideas, often even mutually exclusive. In general, no meaningful comparison between the industrial and the Agile paradigms is possible. It requires the honesty to accept the serious flaws of the old ways, and for leadership and entrepreneurship to embrace the new ways, thereby abandoning the old thinking.

> A gradual shift is factually a status-quo situation that keeps the industrial paradigm intact.

There is overwhelming evidence that the old paradigm doesn't work. But much of the evidence on Agile was anecdotal, personal or relatively minor. The Chaos report of 2011 by the Standish Group marks a turning point. Extensive research was done in comparing traditional projects with projects that used Agile methods. The report shows that an Agile approach to software development results in a much higher yield, even against the old expectations that software must be delivered on time, on budget and with all the promised scope. The report shows that the Agile projects were three times as successful, and there were three times fewer failed Agile projects compared with traditional projects. It is clear that against the right set of expectations, with a focus on active customer collaboration and frequent delivery of *value*, the new paradigm would be performing even better.

Yet, Agile is a choice, not a must. It is one way to improve the software industry. Research shows it is more successful.

*Scrum helps.*

The distinct rules of Scrum help in getting a grip on the new paradigm. The small set of prescriptions, as described in the following chapter, allows immediate action and results in a more fruitful absorption of the new paradigm. Scrum is a tangible way to adopt the Agile paradigm. Via Scrum, people do develop new ways of working; through discovery, experimentation-based learning and collaboration. They enter this new state of being, this state of *agility*; a state of constant change, evolution and improvement.

Nevertheless, despite its practicality, experience shows that adopting Scrum often represents a giant leap. This may be because of uncertainty, letting go of old certainties even if they prove not to be very reliable. It may be because of the time that it takes to make a substantial shift. It may be because of the determination and hard work that is required.

## ■ 1.2    THE ORIGINS OF AGILE

Despite the domination of the plan-driven, industrial views, an
evolutionary approach to software development is not new. Craig Larman
has extensively described the historical predecessors of Agile in his book
'Agile & Iterative Development, A Manager's Guide' (Larman, 2004).

But the official label 'Agile' dates from early 2001, when 17 software
development leaders gathered at the Snowbird ski resort in Utah.
They discussed their views on software development in times when
the failing waterfall approaches were replaced by heavy-weight RUP
implementations, which did not in fact lead to better results than
the traditional processes. These development leaders were following
different paths and methods, each being a distinct implementation of
the new paradigm; Scrum, eXtreme Programming, Adaptive Software
Development, Crystal, Feature Driven Development, DSDM, etc.

The gathering resulted in assigning the label 'Agile' to the common
principles, beliefs and thinking of these leaders and their
methods. They were published as the 'Manifesto for Agile Software
Development' (Beck, et.al., 2001). (See figure 1.3).

---

We are uncovering better ways of developing
software by doing it and helping others do it.
Through this work we have come to value:

**Individuals and interactions** over processes and tools
**Working software** over comprehensive documentation
**Customer collaboration** over contract negotiation
**Responding to change** over following a plan

That is, while there is value in the items on
the right, we value the items on the left more.

---

Figure 1.3 The text of the Manifesto for Agile Software Development

I often overhear the desire "to do Agile". And all too often it is the desire for a magical solution, another silver bullet process that solves all problems. It makes me state that *"Agile does not exist"*. Agile is not one fixed process, method or practice. Agile is the collection of principles that the methods for Agile software development have in common. Agile refers to the mindset, the convictions and the preferences expressed in the Manifesto for Agile Software Development.

The manifesto does help to grasp the ideas underpinning Agile. If you use it as a source to gain a deeper understanding of Agile, then I strongly advise looking at the 12 principles, see: http://agilemanifesto. org/principles.html

## ■ 1.3 DEFINITION OF AGILE

I prefer to describe 'Agile' in terms of the following key characteristics that are common to the portfolio of Agile methods:

- People driven;
- Facilitation;
- Iterative-incremental process;
- Measuring success;
- Change.

### 1.3.1 People driven

Agile software development is not driven by a predictive plan describing how to implement analyzed, designed and architected requirements. Agile acknowledges that requirements cannot be predicted in every possible detail in an upfront way.

Agile is not a process of handing over different types of intermediate deliverables to different specialist departments, where each department performs its specialized work in isolation.

Agile is driven by the continuous *collaboration* of people ranging over all required departments; whether they are called business, IT, marketing, sales, customer service, operations or management.

People are respected for their creativity, intelligence and self-organizing capabilities. People are respected for their ability to understand and resolve a problem without being overloaded with too much ceremony and bureaucracy. A ceremonial overload only replaces this collaborative thinking, innovation and accountability of people with bureaucracy, paper results, handovers and administrative excuses.

People are respected in the time they can spend on their work via the idea of *Sustainable Pace*. Work is organized in such a way that the tempo is sustainable, indefinitely.

### 1.3.2 Facilitation
Agile replaces the traditional command-and-control mechanisms of assigning individuals on a daily basis with executable micro-tasks and totalitarian authorities for invasive control.

Agile teams are *facilitated* by servant-leadership. Boundaries and a context for self-management exist, upon which teams are given objectives and direction. Subtle control emerges from the boundaries.

### 1.3.3 Iterative-incremental process
Agile processes are not free-play approaches. Agile processes are defined and they require high discipline.

Products are created piece by piece ('incremental') with each piece being made up of expansions, improvements and modifications. The built pieces and the total product are frequently revisited ('iterative') to assure overall integrity.

Agile requires explicit attention from all players on quality and excellence. Agile replaces the idea that these can simply be poured into documents and paper descriptions.

### 1.3.4 Measuring success

Progress in software development cannot be measured and guaranteed on the basis of mere compliance with predictive plans and milestones, documents, handovers, signatures, approvals or other ceremonial obligations as is the case in the industrial paradigm.

Agile makes it explicit that success and progress in software development can only be determined by frequently inspecting *working software* and the actual *value* it holds for the people who will have to use it.

It is a natural part of software development that the people having to use the software can never be sure on the usability and usefulness until they actually get their hands on it. No paper documentation or virtual process can replace this.

Agile recognizes no business versus IT discord. The two are needed for success, from the perspective of creating both useable *and* useful software products.

### 1.3.5 Change

Even when requirements and implementations are predicted in an upfront way, they are prone to change. Markets and competitors evolve, users can only know what they want when they get to use it, enterprise strategies change, to name just a few.

Contrary to a predictive process, change is not excluded from the Agile process nor expelled to the ceremonial outskirts of development. New insights, evolving opinions and changed priorities form the living heart of Agile. Agile thrives upon emergence, the emergence of requirements, plans, ideas, architectures and designs. Change is not disruptive because it forms a natural part of the process. Agile encourages change as a source of innovation and improvement.

*What we used to know as 'change' has evaporated.*

## ■ 1.4   THE ITERATIVE-INCREMENTAL CONTINUUM

Every Agile process slices time into time-boxed iterations, periods having a fixed start and end date. There are many advantages to the technique of *time-boxing*, with focus being an important one. This time management technique also ensures regular checks so that the lessons learned can be incorporated from one iteration to the next. The core objective of each iteration is to create builds of valuable, working software at the end of it in order to present this and enable early learning.

Agile software development is driven by *business* and business opportunities. All work is reorganized to respond to and enable that business opportunities can be capitalized on.

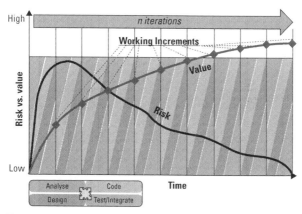

Figure 1.4 Agile value delivery

'Value' is the answer to business opportunities and the overall measure of progress and success. Value is an internal assumption within the organization until the software is actually released to the marketplace. Releasing software on the marketplace is the only way to validate this assumption. Releasing software on the marketplace regularly is the only way to adapt to the feedback and appreciation of the marketplace. This is done in subsequent evolutions of the software. Value is continuously increased across iterations and risk is controlled by consecutively producing working increments based upon defined engineering standards (figure 1.4).

'Risk' also relates to the business perspective. Bear in mind that typically, in an IT context, risk is defined as something technical (*Will the system perform? Is the system scalable?*). But a technical perspective on risk often ignores the fact that the ultimate goal of software development is to provide greater satisfaction to end-users and customers, to ensure that the software products are useful.

Software being usable from a technical perspective is just the beginning.

The software development process should address the risk of not being able to capitalize on unforeseen and previously unknown market opportunities, of not releasing the software product fast enough, of being subject to customer dissatisfaction e.g. by releasing untested software, the risk of releasing features that are not what users expect or appreciate, the risk of lagging behind with regards to the competition.

The Agile development process is organized in such a way so as to mitigate that risk. High-value needs are answered first. Software products, versions and releases are released quickly and frequently. They satisfy existing needs as well as include mind-blowing innovative functions. They get users to pay for the software and optimize the stakeholders' return. They are of high quality in order to minimize maintenance and support.

Agile understands the core purpose of the 'normal' IT activities (in figure 1.4 high-level represented as _A_nalysis, _D_esign, _C_oding and _T_esting/Integration), but breaks the sequential organization of these. To produce shippable software with the right dynamism and get more benefit out of them these activities are structurally re-organized. The goal is to enable flexibility and speed instead of blocking them. In Agile all disciplines are performed in a non-linear, incremental way, in parallel and on a daily basis, by cross-skilled teams with continuous collaboration and negotiation over emergent ideas, techniques and practices.

The goal of such an integrated, cross-functional approach is to build in quality and to prevent defects, rather than attempt to establish quality by a bug hunting approach in a post-development phase. It is imperative to turn the desire to release regularly into the ability to do so. Missing quality cannot be added to a finished product. And delays and budgets tend to grow well out of hand when a lack of quality is identified after the actual creation process has been finished.

Aiming at the real and lasting benefits of Agile software development requires going beyond the borders of the IT departments. The way that Agile not only embraces and incorporates change but even encourages it, is likely to challenge large parts of an organization. But it's more than a must; it's an opportunity to gain leadership. An entire organization will prosper from adopting the Agile mindset of short cycles, frequent results and evolutionary adaptations. The Agile views and approach allow organizations and departments to finally stop trying to predict the unpredictable. Agile practices incorporate dealing with answers, solutions and competing ideas that emerge *while* building software.

It might take some time to experience the fact that the continuous learning innate in Agile actually increases control amidst turbulent enterprise, business and market circumstances. It might take some time to shift management focus away from judgments over the past, e.g. via actuals and time registrations. It might take some time to get confidence out of optimizing and releasing business value through incremental outcomes of the Agile software development process. It might take some time to accept that agility takes time, to accept that agility need not be analyzed, designed and planned before a transformation can take off.

## ■ 1.5   AGILITY CAN'T BE PLANNED

Agility is the state envisioned by moving to Agile processes. Agility is the state of high responsiveness, speed and adaptiveness, while controlling risks. It serves to better deal with the unpredictability so common to the work of software development and to the markets that organizations operate within.

Agility has no purpose if the aforementioned characteristics of responsiveness, speed and adaptiveness don't stretch to the relationship of the organization and its markets, communities and consumers. The adoption of Agile processes is an important foundation for this enterprise agility. From that adoption new processes emerge, together with a new organizational culture of learning, improving and constant adaptation, and restored respect for people.

There are some basic truths that are fundamental to setting the right expectations for the transformation to a state of agility. Introducing Agile methods without accepting these essential truths closes the door to increased agility rather than turning it into a gateway of opportunities:

■  Agility can't be planned;
■  Agility can't be dictated;
■  Agility has no end-state.

A time-planned way to introduce Agile methods introduces unfavorable expectations. Introducing Agile methods is about introducing a new paradigm, and will cause significant organizational change. Existing procedures, departments and functions will be impacted. Such change processes are highly complex and therefore not predictable, even less predictable than creating and sustaining great software products. In a transformation towards an Agile way of working, there is no way of predicting what change needs will be encountered at what point in time, how these will be dealt with and what the exact outcome will be in order to control next steps. There is no way of predicting the pace at which the change will spread and take root.

Agility in itself is much more than following a new process. It is about behavior, it is about *cultural* change. A decision to move to Agile is a decision to leave the old ways behind. It is not only about accepting but also celebrating the fact that agility is living the art of the possible. It requires the courage, honesty and conviction of acting in the moment, acting upon the reality that is exposed by iterative-incremental progress information. Agility is about doing the best possible at every possible moment, constrained by the means we have and facing up to the constraints that arise. A time-planned way for an Agile transformation ignores the essence of Agile, that of dealing with complexity via well-considered steps of experimentation and learning. Time-plans simply extend the old thinking. In general a plan will even slow down the transformation process, because serious delays and waiting times are incorporated.

Time-plans create the illusion of deadlines and a final end-state. Agility has no end-state. Agility is a state of continuous improvement, a state in which each status quo is challenged, by our own will or by external turbulence.

Living the art of the possible engages people and accelerates a transformation as it shapes the future, thrives upon the future and what the future might bring. It's a bright future for organizations that have the vision, the determination and the dedication.

These basic truths must be in the hearts and minds of every person managing, guiding, facilitating or leading a transformation based on the Agile mindset. And even then, it takes time for agility to settle in the hearts and minds of the people impacted by the transformation. After all, people have been instructed in the wrong behavior of the industrial paradigm for 15 to 20 years, or more.

## ◼ 1.6   COMBINING AGILE AND LEAN

For Lean, much like for Agile, it is vital to be aware that it's a set of thinking tools, a collection of interwoven principles that educate, motivate, value and coach people to continuously optimize their work and the way in which they work. The principles of Lean form the levers of a system that people can use to create better products faster, yet in a sustainable and respectful way. It's a system that rewards people for doing the best they can with the means and tools they are given in their actual situation.

There is not one definite, full-blown, one-size-fits-all, unified Lean process, for software development nor for manufacturing, with predefined and prescribed phases, roles, definitions, artifacts, deliverables, etc. A Lean process should be designed upon its principles and thinking, and be constantly tuned to the actual situation. It's about adaptiveness. *The online 'Lean Primer' document of Bas Vodde and Craig Larman does an excellent job of introducing the roots of Lean along with its principles and thinking (Larman & Vodde, 2009).*

### 1.6.1   Major aspects of Lean

#### People

The cornerstone of any system that claims to be Lean are the *people*. And 'people' refers to every possible actor in the whole ecosystem of the Lean product development/build system: customers, workers, teams, suppliers, and managers; internal and external.

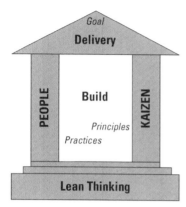

Figure 1.5 Lean principles

All people contribute in their own way and by their own means to building or delivering a product. They collaborate across skills to avoid handovers, delays and waiting time. They autonomously take decisions. They have room to focus on knowledge gathering and constant learning. Managers act as teachers with a *go see* commitment of work-floor presence. They promote the Lean thinking system; help people understand how to reflect on their work, their work results and how to build better products. The whole system embodies the spirit of *Kaizen*, the attitude of continuously thinking about the process, the product and possible improvements. Every member of the whole system can '*stop the line*'[2] if a problem occurs. The root of the problem will be identified and countermeasures will be proposed or installed.

Everyone involved in the value chain works in an integrated way. Relationships with suppliers and external partners are not based upon the traditional approach of large volume purchases, big negotiation rounds and pressuring one another. It's all about building relationships on the sharing of profit (and risk). Lean contracts incorporate mutual growth.

### Waste

When considering the subject of waste, let's mention that *avoiding* waste, via continuous improvement and small step optimizations, is the preferred option. Furthermore, remember that 'waste' refers to process steps, not to getting rid of people.

Obviously, no matter how much attention is paid to avoiding it, waste can and will creep in. The Kaizen spirit drives all people to be committed, aware and critical in their daily work. It's a natural reflex.

A practice to identify structural waste is *Value Stream Mapping*. All steps and phases in the process of going from 'idea' to 'cash' are set out on a timeline. Activities may be labeled as 'valuable' or as 'non-value adding', but possibly also as necessary although not directly value-adding. The *Value Ratio* can be calculated as the ratio of time spent on value-adding activities versus wasteful activities. It's a figure that may serve as a baseline against which improvement can be measured. But, as in all improvement activities, there is no definite end goal, no final state. The improvement itself is the goal.

### Inventory, WIP and flow

Lean strives for continuity and flow. Overproduction of materials disrupts flow and may delay the discovery and resolution of quality issues. But it is also disrespectful as it forces people to do work that may actually never be used. Inventory is costly and makes the organization liable to waste.

Lean says to limit 'Work in Progress' (and costly inventory) by producing only materials when there is a *pull* signal from the next steps in the process in a 'Just in Time' mode. A *kanban* is a physical signal card for this function in manufacturing systems. A kanban is attached to an inventory of parts. It is linked to a level of stock. New parts are only produced when enough materials have been used and the signal card appears.

### 1.6.2 Implementing Lean

Much like with Agile, many organizations struggle with Lean. And on top of that, organizations struggle with the combination of Agile and Lean.

In general, companies refer to organizational problems when expressing a desire for 'Lean'. If they want to become 'Agile' on the other hand, they are most likely referring to problems with software development. However, neither Agile nor Lean offers that one magical, off-the-shelf (silver bullet) solution.

Unfortunately Lean is far too frequently assumed to be limited to *eliminate waste*. Just picking out that one element from the toolbox is already an undesirable over-focus on just one aspect, instead of looking at the whole. It gets even worse when the principle itself is broken, and when 'elimination' is applied to *people* and not as a means to *improve*. The highly popular management sport of 'cost cutting' tends to twist this important Lean practice into designating people's work as an 'overhead', i.e. non-valuable. The underlying signal says that the people who are doing that work are waste and ... disposable.

From that popular misconception and its all too limited perspective on Lean, it is a long journey to build up an understanding that Lean is primarily about respecting people in order to optimize value and quality. That Lean is more about the *context* in which people can prosper in order to perform, than about continuously over-stressing the need for results and performance. It invokes the difficult exercise of letting go of 'command and control', of big boss behavior, micro-management, over-allocation and nano-assignments.

It is a long way from this misconception to an understanding of Lean beyond the formal practices, an understanding of Lean as a thinking context with no definite end state, with people continuously reflecting on their daily work and self-improving.

*Agile can help.*

There are more than just a few similarities between Agile and Lean that are worthwhile exploring. Some management or governance philosophies should not be mixed up because this will result in a blurry amalgam and the unique flavor of the ingredients will get lost in the mix, as will the benefits. But, as far as Agile and Lean are concerned, I don't only believe that Lean and Agile *can* be combined, the combination of Lean management principles with Agile product development thinking, as a total outcome, will actually result in a more powerful mix.

Lean and Agile are truly *blending* philosophies. Lean thrives on a powerful but typical mindset. Agile has distinct practices that not only match the main Lean principles extremely well, but even form a very tangible implementation of them for software development purposes.

### 1.6.3    The blending philosophies of Lean and Agile

I have published a more detailed paper on this subject with the same title, 'The Blending Philosophies of Lean and Agile' (Verheyen, 2011), which can be found at www.scrum.org/Community/Community-Publications. Here we will show just some of the clear strategies in Agile that align it with Lean:

- *Potentially unused inventories:* Detailed requirements, hard-coded plans, designs, etc. form a liability in software development, and not an asset, because they represent potentially unused work. Agile avoids producing these upfront in every possible detail. If the potential point of implementation of identified work is still some time away, the chances are quite high that this will not be implemented. The exact expectations may change in the meantime, or experience from intermediate implementation and releases may indicate better ways of implementing the distant requirement. Only the upcoming, highest ordered work is detailed more fully, as it is this that will be worked on next. And even then a team will only *pull* in the amount of work they deem feasible for an iteration, and start building it based on progressive learning and continuous improvement, even on a daily base.

- *Partially done work:* Work that is not completely finished, 'almost there, I just need a little more time'-type of work, is a known, important type of waste in software development. In an Agile process the goal of each iteration is to produce a *working* piece of product. No partial work is included in the software at the end of an iteration. The overall Kaizen thinking, and its explicit daily *Inspect & Adapt* implementation in Agile, helps team in not taking up new work while undone work remains in the iteration. Time-boxing is a time-management technique that helps teams focus on finishing work.

- *Feature usage:* Research has shown that barely 20% of the features included in a product built in a traditional way are regularly used (Standish, 2002). Unused or under-used functions thus represent an enormous waste of effort and budget, both in terms of developing and maintaining them. Active collaboration with people who know and represent the customer prevents the production of unwanted or invaluable requirements, and helps a team focus on a minimal set of features that may be released. The focus on 'wanted' requirements saves not only development budget, it also ensures that future maintenance and support costs can be kept much lower. And the iterative-incremental process allows teams to regularly adapt the product based upon an effective appreciation of the delivered value and also capitalize on new value expectations.

Agile has clear strategies for continuous improvement, thereby leveraging the Kaizen spirit:

- The work plan of an Agile team is checked daily and updated;
- At the end of an iteration the software that has been produced is verified to gather feedback, remarks, improvements and enhancements;
- The process, the way the teams work, collaborate, communicate and undertake implementation, is verified at its latest point via an iteration retrospective.

Agile *optimizes the whole* by demanding that customers or their proxies express and order work, and take an active part in the development process for clarification and functional trade-offs even during implementation. All implementation skills are available within a team to turn their ideas, options and requirements into working software in a single iteration.

Agile shortens cycle times by optimizing the value stream through the prevention of traditional waiting activities like handovers and external decisions. There are no macro handovers, i.e. handovers across departments and organizations, which typically occur in a sequential organization of work with large blocks of specialized work packages. But there are also no micro handovers, i.e. handovers between individuals and within a team, given the collective accountability of the team.

In general, the strategies and principles of Agile are consistent with, and even leveraging, all major Lean principles, as I've indicated in figure 1.6.

| Lean | Agile |
|---|---|
| Respect for People | Self-organizing Teams |
| Kaizen | Inspect & adapt, short feedback cycles |
| Prevent/eliminate Waste | No unused specs, architecture or infrastructure |
| Pull inventory (Kanban) | Estimates reflect team capacity |
| Visual management | Information radiators |
| Built-in Quality | Definition of Done, Engineering standards |
| Customer Value | Active Business Collaboration |
| Optimizing the whole | Whole Team Together (incl. stakeholders) |
| Deliver fast | Timeboxed iterations with working Increments |
| The manager-teacher | The facilitating servant-leader |

Figure 1.6 The consistency in principles of Lean and Agile

Notes

[1] Frederick Taylor (1856-1915) was an American engineer who is best known for his research into ways to optimize the productivity, efficiency and the cost of labor. He promoted enforced standardization and the enforced adoption of systematic methods and practices. Control lay exclusively with management, with workers being there only to carry out the work (Source: http://en.wikipedia.org/wiki/Frederick_Winslow_Taylor).

[2] This refers to the Toyota car manufacturing origins of Lean, where every person at the production line is entitled to stop the line when problems, defects or a lack of quality are detected.

## 2 Scrum

### ■ 2.1 THE HOUSE OF SCRUM

The house of Scrum (figure 2.1) is a warm house. It's a house where people are W E L C O M E.

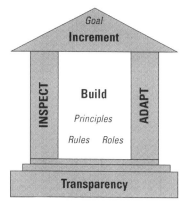

Figure 2.1 The house of Scrum

In the house of Scrum people from different backgrounds, in different roles, with different skills, talents and personalities work, learn and improve together. The house of Scrum is an inclusive house of warm, open and collaborative relationships.

The house of Scrum knows no 'versus'. Barriers are removed, instead of being maintained or created. There's no business versus IT in the house of Scrum, no team versus the world, no Product Owner versus Development Team, no coding versus support, no testers versus programmers, no my team versus your team, no Scrum Master versus the organization. The house of Scrum offers an open view on the world. The house of Scrum is a great and energizing place where product development prospers from the combined, creative intelligence of self-organizing people.

The house of Scrum helps to stay away from rigid behavior. Its inhabitants, their teams and the ecosystems in which they operate show flexibility to better deal with uncertainty, internal tensions and external pressure on the ecosystem. They probe, sense and adapt at all levels; at the strategy and tactical levels, from requirements to plans to objectives to markets to technology.

Scrum is an enabler for building software products better and faster. But, most of all, it restores energy and work pleasure for all of the involved players; from those who create the products, to those who have a stakeholder interest in the product being created, to those who consume the product and its services, to all who co-create it with opinions, feedback and appreciation.

## ■ 2.2 SCRUM, WHAT'S IN A NAME?

The term 'Scrum' was first used by Hirotaka Takeuchi and Ikujiro Nonaka, two acknowledged management thinkers, in their ground-breaking 1986 paper 'The New New Product Development Game' (Takeuchi & Nonaka, 1986). With the term 'Scrum' they referred to the game of rugby to stress the importance of *teams* and some analogies between a team sport like rugby and being successful in the game of new product development. The research described in their paper showed that outstanding performance in the development of new, complex products is achieved when teams, as small and self-organizing units of people, are fed with *objectives*, not with tasks. The best performing teams are those that are given direction within which they have room to devise their own tactics on how to best head towards their joint objective. Teams require autonomy to achieve excellence.

... as in Rugby, the ball gets passed within the team as it moves as a unit up the field. Takeuchi Nonaka (1986). *The New New Product Development Game*

Figure 2.2 A Scrum in the game of rugby

Jeff Sutherland and Ken Schwaber conceived the Scrum process for Agile software development in the early 90's. They presented Scrum for the first time in 1995 at the Oopsla[1] conference in Austin, Texas (US) (Schwaber, 1995; Sutherland, 1995).

They inherited the name 'Scrum' from the paper by Takeuchi and Nonaka. The Scrum framework for software development implements the principles described in this paper for developing and sustaining complex *software* products. If teams are only instructed to carry out executable tasks and their capacity in hours is pre-filled with such tasks, team members suffer from a narrowed mind. They are restricted from looking and thinking beyond the prescriptions, even if reality or experience shows that the prescribed solution is difficult to achieve or is suboptimal. They lose openness for better solutions, for solutions that are not dictated and that are a better fit to the actual demand given change, proven findings and current circumstances. Their only focus is to deliver what was instructed without considering conflicting ideas and options, without dealing with the natural form of instability typical to product development and technological discovery. The industrial mode to direct people as if they were robots impedes the rise of the collective intelligence of a team, thereby limiting their work results to mediocre levels.

We have already pointed out the remarkable similarities between Lean and Agile in section 1.6. However, there is also a connection between Scrum and Lean via 'The New New Product Development Game', and the term 'Scrum'.

The authors of the 'The New New Product Development Game' paper are very familiar with, and are proponents of, Lean. Over the course of their careers and assignments they have studied and described well-known Lean companies. Yet they never use the term 'Lean'.

In their paper, Takeuchi and Nonaka wanted to describe the pumping heart of Lean, and called it 'Scrum', as a differentiator in terms of complex product development. The viewpoint is that an organization is unlikely to benefit from any so-called 'Lean' practice for developing complex products if this pumping heart is not present and only the practices surrounding it are installed. Unfortunately this is the case for many Lean implementations, so the authors preferred to stress the need for the heart and soul of the system and take away the focus on the surrounding management practices.

So, they opted not to mention Lean, and focused instead on its engine, i.e. Scrum.

Furthermore they confirmed that 'Lean' had become synonymous with the *management* practices of the Toyota Production System. For this reason also, they barely talked of Lean.

> *'Scrum should be at the heart of every implementation of Lean.'*
> *Jeff Sutherland (Sutherland, 2011).*

## ■ 2.3   IS THAT A GORILLA I SEE OVER THERE?

Evolutionary practices for software development have been around for a long time (Larman, 2004). The Scrum process for Agile software development has been available and documented since 1995. The Agile movement was formed in 2001. This new paradigm for the software industry has taken root and its adoption is increasing steadily.

A widely accepted model to assess and represent the degree of adoption of a technological product or service is Geoffrey Moore's expanded version of the 'Technology Adoption Life Cycle' (TALC) (Moore, 1999; Wiefels 2002). See figure 2.3.

Geoffrey Moore had observed the difference in the adoption pattern for technology products or services representing a *disruptive* new paradigm causing a discontinuity in innovation. Moore confirmed the general phases and audiences to be in line with the adoption of products representing a continuous evolution. But after the phase of *Early Market* Moore observed and added to the model a period of stagnation. It is a period where adoption stalls. An unpredictable time passes by before entering the next phase of adoption, the *Bowling Alley*.

And some products never even get out of this stand-still and simply disappear. Moore called this period the *Chasm*.

During the highly turbulent phase of *Bowling Alley* a *gorilla* is formed, a market leader. In the subsequent phases, until the disappearance of the product off the market, it turns out that market leaders, in general, are difficult to overthrow.

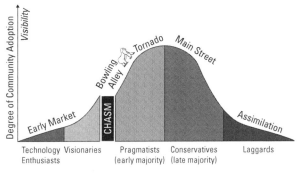

Figure 2.3 The Technology Adoption Life Cycle

In addition to the use of Agile for the development of new, possibly disruptive, technological products, Agile in itself is absolutely a new, and clearly disruptive, paradigm on the technology market.

The years since the emergence of the first Agile processes (*avant la lettre*) and the official establishment of the term 'Agile' in 2001 marked the *Early Market* phase of Agile.

Around 2007-2008 there was a general consensus that Agile was crossing the Chasm. Up to that point evidence on Agile was mostly anecdotal and generally based on individual enterprise adoptions, technology cases and personal storytelling. This is typical of the phases of the technology adoption life cycle in question. It is equally typical that mostly enthusiasts and visionaries were attracted by it. But once the Chasm was crossed, Agile also became attractive to a broader audience, the audience of *Early Pragmatists*. They typically look at the business advantages of a less proven paradigm, and compare its problem-solving capabilities to the existing paradigm. Yahoo! is an important example of a large company transitioning to Agile, and documenting their experiences in 2008 (Benefield, 2008).

In Q3 2009, Forrester Research and Dr. Dobb's (Hammond & West, 2009) conducted a survey amongst IT professionals worldwide including an investigation into the type of "*methodology (that) most closely reflects the development process you are currently using*". Perhaps surprisingly to a number of people, 36% of the participants indicated that they were doing Agile, while only 13% confirmed to be following a waterfall process[2]. This was an important formal confirmation of the common perception that the use of Agile had indeed gradually been overtaking the waterfall model.

In April 2012, Forrester Research (Giudice, 2011) published the results of a survey on the global adoption of Agile for software application development noting that "the IT industry is (...) widely adopting Agile" and that the adoption of Agile is not limited to small enterprises. Large organizations form a substantial part of the companies moving to Agile. Forrester had also found that "Shorter iterations and Scrum practices are the most common Agile practices" and that Scrum is one of the most common development approaches. This confirmed the widespread finding that Scrum is the most commonly applied method for Agile software development. Forrester thereby validated the results of the yearly 'State of Agile Development' surveys conducted by VersionOne (2011, 2013).

Although the adoption of Scrum is not typical or limited to a specific economic sector, Forrester found the financial services industry to have the highest adoption of Agile methods. This is striking as large financial institutions are by their nature very risk averse. And they are now adopting Scrum successfully (Verheyen & Arooni, 2012).

> Scrum is the de facto standard against which to measure, to oppose or to join. Scrum has emerged as the gorilla of the Agile family of methods for software development.

## ■ 2.4 FRAMEWORK, NOT METHODOLOGY

Scrum, with its roots in new product development theory, is designed to help teams create and sustain complex software products in turbulent circumstances via self-organization. Scrum implements the scientific method of empiricism to better deal with the complexity and unpredictability of software development. Scrum replaces the industrial, plan-driven paradigm with well-considered, opportunistic experimentation. The content of the Scrum framework has been consciously limited to a bare minimal set of mandatory elements, so that each element becomes essential. Breaking Scrum's base design by leaving out one or more elements is likely to cover up problems, instead of revealing them.

The purpose of empiricism via Scrum is to help people perform *inspections* & *adaptations* upon *transparency* of the work being undertaken. Scrum builds in frequent reality checks to assure best possible decisions. Scrum helps to adjust, adapt, change and gain flexibility. The rules, principles and roles of the framework, as described in the Scrum Guide (Schwaber & Sutherland, 2013), serve this purpose.

Scrum, through its minimalistic design, has no exhaustive and formal prescriptions on how to design and plan the behavior of all software development actors, nor does it lay out their expected behavior against time in designs and plans, let alone how these designs and plans must be documented, maintained and stored. Scrum has no rules for upfront predictions of document types and deliverables to be produced. Neither does Scrum instruct the exact time of their production. Instead of installing, thriving and relying on handovers, toll gates and control meetings, Scrum de-installs them as a major source of delays, waste and disrespect.

Methodologies, by design, are composed of stringent and mandatory sequences of steps, processes and procedures, implementing predefined algorithms and executers for each step, process or procedure. This holds the promise of success when the prescriptions are followed. As such, 'methodologies' aspire to replace the creativity, autonomy and intellectual powers of people with components like phases, tasks, must-do practices and patterns, executive techniques and tools. Practice and research shows that obedience to the methodology only serves to ensure formal coverage for blame, not the success of working results (Standish, 2011). Methodologies depend on high degrees of predictability to have a high yield. Software development does not have that high degree of predictability.

Scrum is the opposite of such a big collection of interwoven mandatory components and maximal set of complete prescriptions. Scrum is not a methodology. Scrum replaces a pre-programmed algorithmic approach with a heuristic one, with respect for people and self-organization in order to deal with unpredictability and to solve complex problems.

If and when Scrum is referred to as a 'process', it is certainly not a repeatable process. That's often a challenge to explain, because the term 'process' typically invokes a sense of algorithmic and predictable steps, repeatable actions and enforceable top-down control; the sort of expectations that are typical for ... a methodology.

If referred to as a 'process', then Scrum is a *servant* process, not a *commanding* process. What works best for all involved players and their processes at work, emerges from the use of Scrum, not from a dictate by Scrum's definition. Players discover the work required to close the gap between an inspected intermediate result and an envisioned outcome. Scrum is a process that helps surface the most effective process, practices and structures. Scrum helps discover a way of working that is continuously adaptable to everybody's actual context and current circumstances. Therefore, we prefer to call Scrum... a framework.

The framework of Scrum sets the bounded environments for action, and leaves it to the people to take action, decide on the best possible action within those boundaries.

## ■ 2.5 PLAYING THE GAME

The goal of Scrum, as a *framework* for Agile software development, is to optimize and control the creation of *valuable* software in turbulent enterprise, organizational, business and market circumstances.

The game board of Scrum (figure 2.4) shows the elementary elements and principles of Scrum, all that's minimally required to optimally play the game.

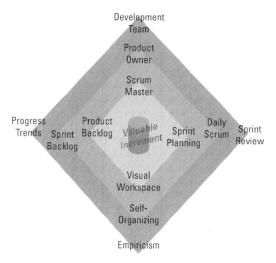

Figure 2.4 The Scrum game board

Scrum requires great discipline from its players, but still leaves much room for personal creativity and context-specific expansions. The rules of the game are based upon respect for the people-players through a subtle and balanced distribution of responsibilities. Respecting the rules of the game, not taking shortcuts on rules and roles, nor short-circuiting the empirical grounds of the game, deliver the most joys and greatest benefits.

The Scrum game board shows the players, the artifacts, the events and the main principles of the game of Scrum. Let's take a closer look at the rules that bind these elements together.

### 2.5.1 Players and accountabilities

Agile methods are driven by a sense of business opportunism. The time-management technique of time-boxing all work allows the players to quickly respond to new opportunities and adapt to any changes and evolutions.

Scrum organizes its players into Scrum Teams. A Scrum Team consists of three roles, where each role complements the other roles in accountability, thereby turning collaboration into the key to success:

- A Product Owner;
- A Development Team;
- A Scrum Master.

The *Product Owner*, a one-person player role, brings the business perspective of the software product to a Scrum Team. The Product Owner represents all stakeholders, internal and external, to the *Development Team*, a multi-person player role. Although a Product Owner may have various strategic product management tasks outside of the Scrum Team, it is important that the Product Owner actively engages with the other players of the team regularly and repeatedly.

The Product Owner assures with the Development Team that a *Product Backlog* exists. The Product Owner manages the Product Backlog based on the product vision as a long-term view of the road ahead. Product vision captures *why* the product is being built.

The Product Backlog shows all of the work actually envisioned for the product that's being created and sustained. This work may comprise functional and non-functional expectations, enhancements, fixes, patches, ideas, updates and other requirements. If anybody wants to know what work is identified and planned for the product they only have to look at the Product Backlog.

The Product Owner expresses the business expectations and ideas captured in the Product Backlog to the team, and orders the items in the Product Backlog to optimize the value being delivered. The Product Owner also manages the game budget to optimize the balance of value, effort and time for the represented stakeholders.

The *Development Team* self-organizes to perform all end-to-end development activities required to turn items from the Product Backlog, expressed and ordered by the Product Owner, into releasable software. 'Development' applies to all work undertaken by the Development Team within a Sprint, such as test cases, all testing activities, programming code, documentation, integration work, release activities, etc. It covers all work necessary to guarantee that the *Increment* of product at the end of each Sprint is usable and that it technically can be released to the users and consumers of the product or service. The criteria that need to be met to do so, and thus also drive the development work to be undertaken by the Development Team, is often captured in a 'definition of done'.

The Development Team also has a set of 'Engineering Standards' that describes how the implementation is being performed. This is required to guarantee the level of quality needed to ship regularly. And it provides the right transparency to the way the game is being played.

The Development Team sets the cost or effort indication on Product Backlog items. The Development Team selects the amount of work it assumes it can handle in a Sprint at the start of that particular Sprint. The evolving effort indications on Product Backlog can be compared with proven experience to make a *forecast* of Product Backlog for a Sprint.

The *Scrum Master*, a one-person player role, facilitates the Product
Owner and the Development Team during the game. The Scrum
Master teaches, coaches and mentors the Scrum Team, and also the
organization, in understanding, respecting and knowing how to
play the game of Scrum. The Scrum Master makes sure the rules of
the game are well understood and that any elements that hinder or
block the team in its progress are removed. Such elements are called
*Impediments* in Scrum.

The Scrum Master induces the continual desire to become better
players. The Scrum Master implements Scrum by helping others to use
Scrum.

### 2.5.2  Time

The time-boxed iterations in the game of Scrum are called *Sprints*.
Sprints allow the Development Team to focus on achieving the next
game level, the *Sprint Goal*, with minimal external disruptions.

All of the work in Scrum is organized in Sprints (figure 2.5). Scrum
does not typecast Sprints as the goal of *each* Sprint is to deliver a
valuable piece of working software, a (product) *Increment*. A Sprint's
duration is never more than four weeks and typically takes one to four
weeks.

As a container event, the Sprint encapsulates the Scrum meetings,
where every meeting is a time-boxed event and is an opportunity to
adapt to changing conditions:

- Sprint Planning;
- Daily Scrum;
- Sprint Review;
- Sprint Retrospective.

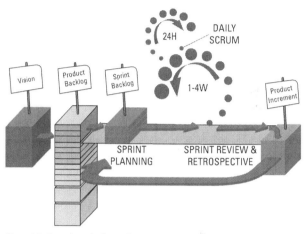

Figure 2.5 Overview of a Scrum Sprint

Every Sprint begins with *Sprint Planning* where the Development
Team pull work into the Sprint from the actual Product Backlog.
The team selects the amount of work it deems feasible for the Sprint
against the expectations of what it takes to make it releasable. The
selected work is a *forecast* that represents the insights that the team
has at the time of selection. The Development Team might look at the
amount of work they have, on average, completed in past Sprints and
compare this to their capacity for the upcoming Sprint, to slightly
increase the accuracy of the forecast. The views of the Product Owner
are respected, and additional details are discussed with the Product
Owner during this meeting.

The selected work, the forecast, is designed, analyzed and elaborated
into a list of actionable development work, the *Sprint Backlog*. After
the expiration of the time-box of the event, or possibly sooner,
the Development Team starts upon this work plan that has been

collaboratively created. Sprint Planning never takes more than eight hours.

To manage and follow up on its development work the Development Team holds a short, 15 minutes, daily meeting called the *Daily Scrum*. The meeting serves as a right-time planning event. The plan with the upcoming work of the team is optimized for achieving the Sprint Goal based upon the actual progress within the Sprint. The adaptation is captured in an update of the Sprint Backlog. The actual progress on the Sprint Backlog is visualized, based upon the amount of remaining work. If the actual progress impacts upon the forecast, the Development Team consults with the Product Owner.

As the Sprint progresses, an Increment of the product emerges from the team's collaborative work. At the end of the Sprint, the Increment is inspected in a *Sprint Review* to check on the functional fitness to release it. If the Product Owner, as sole representative of all stakeholders, deems the Increment useful then the Increment is released without delay.

The Product Owner furthermore maintains a high level of transparency by presenting Product Backlog evolutions during the Sprint against the long-term product vision. While reviewing the product Increment all players are likely to discover changes and receive feedback and evolutionary insights from the inspection. These are processed into the Product Backlog for future implementation, while understanding that the exact implementation date depends on the Product Owner's ordering and the team's sustainable progress. A Sprint Review never takes more than four hours.

The Sprint is concluded with a *Sprint Retrospective* in which the Scrum Team inspects, and reflects upon, the complete, *well*, 'process'. The meeting covers all aspects of the work, i.e. technology, social aspects, the Scrum process, development practices, product quality, etc. The meeting is basically about establishing what went well, where there is room for improvement and what experiments might be usefully conducted in order to learn and build a better product.

As part of continuous improvement the Scrum Team agrees on preservations, adjustments, experiments and improvements for the next Sprint. A Sprint Retrospective never takes more than three hours.

> Scrum only knows Sprints, and the goal of each Sprint is to deliver a piece of working software, an Increment of the product. Working software is considered the only measure of progress.

The Sprint length is kept steady over several Sprints for reasons of consistency. It is the heartbeat of development and it's useful for the team to understand how much work can be done during a Sprint.

This amount of work is sometimes expressed as *Velocity*. Velocity is an indication of the amount of work a team was able to create in past Sprints. Velocity is the sum of effort or cost units that were completed in a Sprint and is typical to one team, and one team's composition.

The Sprint length is right-sized to capitalize on emerging and previously unforeseen business opportunities. The collaborative Sprint Review provides the Product Owner with the best possible information on which to decide whether the Product will be shipped, and how additional Sprints can further improve the value of the product taking into account a balance of risk, effort, budget and cohesion.

The Sprint length may also depend on how long a Team can work without consulting with stakeholders at the Sprint Review. The Sprint Review is an opportunity to adapt to new strategic directions.

A team will suffer from reduced learning and adaptation opportunities when not consulting with stakeholders, markets, business evolutions and new strategies at least every 30 days. Sprints may be shorter than four weeks, but never longer. Modern software development occurs in highly complex and unpredictable circumstances.

### 2.5.3  Tracking progress

Overall progress of work is tracked and visualized, in order to create progress *trends* that add predictability to uncertainty.

In order to continuously measure and adapt to reality and achieve the best predictability possible, taking into account the levels of complexity, the remaining work is re-estimated regularly and honestly:

- *Sprint progress:* Within a Sprint, progress is tracked on a daily basis. The Sprint Backlog always holds the most realistic plan and estimates of the work remaining to implement the Sprint Goal.
- *Product progress:* The progress indication at the level of the Product Backlog is updated and reviewed at a minimum at the Sprint Review meeting. The Product Owner may package Product Backlog items into tentative releases. The proven progress of past Sprints gives the Product Owner and its stakeholders a forecasted delivery date for releases, individual features or feature sets.

The classic Scrum approach to visualize progress is a *Burn-down chart*, a graph showing the evolution of total remaining work (figure 2.6).

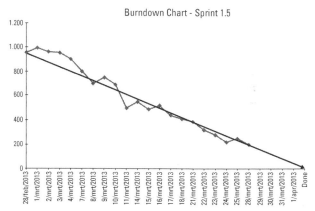

Figure 2.6 Example of a Sprint burn-down chart

However, the team decides on the best way to represent progress. This may be a burn-down chart, a physical Scrum board, a burn-up chart (e.g. in value), or it could be a cumulative flow diagram (figure 2.7).

### 2.5.4 The value of the Product Backlog

It is often said that the Product Backlog must capture all requirements. However, the value of the Product Backlog lies not in completeness, precision, detail or perfection. The value of the Product Backlog lies in transparency, in making clear what work needs to be done in order to create a minimally viable and valuable product (or product Increment). The Product Backlog brings out into the open all work, development, compliances, and constraints that a team has to deal with in order to create releasable software.

Product Backlog is an ordered list of ideas, features and options to bring an envisioned software product to life, and to sustain and grow it. The list is bound to include all functionalities and features, but

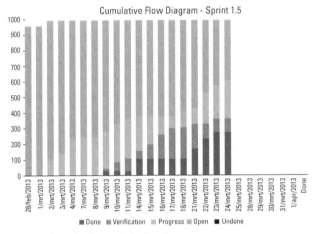

Figure 2.7 Example of a cumulative flow diagram

naturally also includes fixes, maintenance work, architectural work, work to be spent on security, scalability, stability and performance, etc. At the time of the creation of an item on the Product Backlog, the item is supposedly valuable for a customer.

Every item on the Product Backlog holds just enough detail to make it clear what the value represents. An item is intentionally incomplete to encourage additional and explicit discussion over it. Each item is a placeholder for discussion at the appropriate time.

The Product Owner has accountability for the Product Backlog. But this won't prevent the Product Owner from taking into account the technical and development input from the Development Team. Neither will it prevent the Product Owner from taking into account dependencies, non-functional requirements and organizational expectations.

The Product Backlog is gradually refined, thereby introducing
incremental requirements management over the product (figure 2.8).

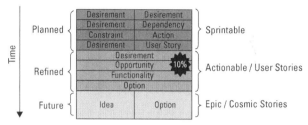

Figure 2.8 Incremental evolution of Product Backlog

As development progresses, the Product Backlog is refined, adjusted
and updated. The Product Backlog is continuously ordered and
re-ordered by the Product Owner. The items are regularly refined in
conjunction with the Development Team. Experience shows that 10%
is a sensible average of the overall time incurred on a Sprint to spend
on Product Backlog refinement.

The Product Owner looks to balance the needs of all stakeholders,
internal and external, who are to be represented in the Scrum Team.
Continuously adhering to 'just enough' descriptions and designs of
the work, i.e. leaving out unnecessary details, ensures that no excessive
money and time is wasted if the item ultimately isn't created or is
implemented in a different fashion.

The level of description and detail of a Product Backlog item lies
somewhere between what used to be a desire and what used to be a
requirement. A 'desire' is too fuzzy to work on and a requirement
is over-specified and over-detailed. Over-specification in software
development impedes the optimal use of technology, blocks the ability
to capitalize on synergies between different functions and is a waste of

money in situations of even minimal turbulence or change. Therefore the term 'desirement' is well suited to a Product Backlog item.

Desirements move through in their ordering from Product Backlog via Sprint Backlog into Increments of working product. While the ordering of the Product Backlog depends upon a complex combination of factors like cost/effort, dependencies, priority, cohesion and consistency, it is essential to have a view on the value.

Core factors for a Product Backlog item are cost and value:

- *Cost:* The cost, or effort, of a Product Backlog item is generally expressed as the relative size of the item. Past Sprints show a team how much work, expressed in effort or cost, can be transformed on average into a working Increment during a Sprint. Upon this empirical given, an expectation can be created of when an item on the actual Product Backlog might become available as part of an evolving product. It gives predictability, yet does not move into the realm of predictions given that any such expectation is constrained by today's knowledge and circumstances.
- *Value:* An important principle of Agile is "*to satisfy the customer through early and continuous delivery of valuable software*" (Beck et al., 2001). Without an attribute for (business) value on Product Backlog items, a Product Owner has no idea of how much value a feature, an idea or a feature set presumably brings to the customer whom he/she represents within the Scrum Team. Value will depend on the type of enterprise and the product and market expectations. The value of a Product Backlog item can be indirect, in it that not picking up a Product Backlog item might undercut the value of the system or even the organization, or that not pulling it may produce negative value.

The notion of value helps Product Owners and their stakeholders move away from the (false idea of) perfection of a total product that must be completely built before even considering its release. The focus shifts to a minimal marketable product release and the minimal work it takes to bring effective value to the marketplace. Product Backlog can be used to group items, features and non-functional requirements into cohesive feature sets.

> Product Backlog is all the plan Scrum requires, its 'desirements' hold all the information needed for predictability about scope and time. A Product Backlog item needs the right attributes to be ordered, more than just prioritized.

### 2.5.5 The importance of done

In a definition of 'done' the conditions are expressed that need to be met by an Increment of product in order for it to be 'shippable'. It is an overview of all the activities, criteria, tasks and work that need to have been performed on a working piece of software in order to be able to release it into production.

The definition of done is essential to fully understand the work needed to create a releasable Increment and for the inspection of that Increment at the Sprint Review. The definition of done serves the transparency required in Scrum in terms of the work to be done and the work actually done.

The prefix 'potentially' is, however, added to 'shippable Increment'. This refers to the Product Owner's accountability to decide upon the actual release of an Increment; a decision that will likely be based on business cohesion and functional usefulness as observed during the Sprint Review. Yet, the Product Owner's shipping decision should not be constrained by 'development' work, hence all work required to achieve the level of done is performed before the Sprint Review meeting in the Sprint.

The empiricism of Scrum only functions well with transparency. Transparency requires common standards to work against and to inspect upon. The definition of done sets the standard for *releasable*, and should be known by all players. Transparency means not only visible, but also understandable. The content of the definition of done should be self-explanatory.

Through the definition of done, quality is at the heart of what Scrum Teams do. No undone work is part of the Increment. No undone work is put into production. *Ever.* From the inspection of the Increment based upon the definition of done at the Sprint Review, the collaborative conversation might include quality, and requirements with regards to the definition of quality in the organization. This helps the team consider the definition of done at the subsequent Sprint Retrospective. The self-organizing drive of the Development Team will include all that's actually possible, and more, take into account the feedback from the stakeholders.

Primary ownership of the definition of done lies with the Development Team, in the same way that primary ownership of Product Backlog lies with the Product Owner. The Development Team does all the hard work related to delivering working software that complies to the definition of done. A definition of done can't be forced upon a Development Team. Neither can it be cut short by forces outside of the Development Team. The Development Team will include its own development standards and will obviously incorporate the functional or business quality expectations from the Product Owner. The Development Team will also include general, organizational expectations and compliance (from the development, engineering, quality or operations areas).

Decisions over the definition of done will depend on the presence of the skills, authorizations and availability of external systems, services and interfaces. Although dependencies are typically managed via ordering of the Product Backlog, a Development Team prefers to make progress. The team is likely to include stubs and simulators for non-available systems or non-resolved technical dependencies. But all parties remain aware that it is not really done, as in releasable. It increases the independence of the team but does not remove the dependence. There is an unpredictable amount of work hidden in the system and it must be performed at some point in order to have shippable software. In the mean time the Product Owner is blocked from making the decision on whether or not to actually release. Fortunately the Sprint Review reveals this information to stakeholders too, so the chances are greater that appropriate actions will be taken within the organization.

> The definition of done stresses the importance of seizing the opportunity to ship by doing all of the work required to capitalize on an opportunity within a Sprint.

## ■ 2.6  CORE PRINCIPLES OF SCRUM

The Scrum game board (figure 2.4) not only shows the formally prescribed elements of Scrum but also three principles of Scrum that I consider to be main principles and which I will elaborate on here:

- Shared visual workspace;
- Self-organization;
- Empirical process control.

### 2.6.1 Shared visual workspace

Teams, in order to function properly and grow into a mature and performing state, need a workspace they can share for their daily work. The team will organize the workspace to optimize communication and collaboration. This removes barriers – physical or mental – that obstruct the flow of information. The shared workspace facilitates the team and its members in making fast and committed decisions. It's not mandatory but obviously physical co-location is most optimal from a team dynamics perspective. But even when not working co-located, a team needs a shared workspace, utilizing modern communication facilities.

Within the workspace a team should look to focus on value-adding activities. All overhead and administrative work is kept to a bare minimum. This includes the storage of information. Teams require fast access to all team information, in order to create, maintain and share it, and speed up all decisions that will be made upon it. It's why teams prefer to apply *visual management* techniques. The shared workspace is probably filled with *information radiators* (Cockburn, 2002)[3]. Information radiators limit the time it takes to convey information and focus on the team as a unit, which is crucial when considering software development.

A task overview, team definitions, standards and agreements, process artifacts and progress trends are all made accessible and visible within the shared workspace by posting them on the room walls; on white boards, flip charts or other means. This is not limited to the strict process artifacts, but also includes all information the team deems appropriate to visualize, such as designs and models, impact analyses, impediments, the definition of done, the engineering standards etc.

Upon entering the room all of the information is readily available, the room radiates it towards the interested reader. The reader is not forced to enter electronic systems, get authorizations, authenticate, search for it, search for the most recent version of it, or even enquire about it. Scrum Teams maintain all crucial information this way to *share* it within and beyond the team members, and use it to inspect and adapt.

The information is not static. It constantly reflects the current state of affairs, where the current state might be used to project expectations of the future, like burn-down charts.

A shared visual workspace optimizes transparency and reduces the length of information exchange drastically.

### 2.6.2 Self-organization
Scrum thrives on the daily collaboration of the three peer roles within a Scrum Team. Each role has clear accountabilities within the team as well as towards the organization. The Scrum Team and within it the Development Team are self-organizing units of people.

Self-organization is not just the degree of freedom that is allowed. Self-organization is not about delegation, self-organization *is*, it happens. Self-organization is not about enabling or empowerment, there is no higher authority that grants it. The ability to actually self-organize requires the removal of many existing barriers that prevent people from communicating, achieving insights and collaborating. There's the role for external authority; facilitating teams by removing organizational or procedural barriers.

Self-organization is not about anarchy or limitless freedom. Self-organization has and requires boundaries, boundaries within which self-organizations happens. The Scrum rules are one of the primary boundaries within which a team organizes its own work:

■ The Development Team collaboratively selects work that is ordered and expressed by the Product Owner, collaboratively creates actionable activities for their forecast and re-plans the work on a daily basis within a time-boxed Sprint to optimize the team's output.

■ The Product Owner interacts with stakeholders and product management to identify the most valuable work, and relies on the cross-functional Development Team for the actual delivery of it in Increments of software product. Stakeholders help in shaping the future product at every Sprint Review.

■ The Scrum Master has no interest in scope, budget, delivery or tasks but coaches and facilitates the complete ecosystem in using Scrum to manage them.

People organized in teams have the highest cohesion, deepest trust and most effective interconnections when the size of the team numbers around seven. Although Scrum sets the expectation of Development Team size between three and nine, there's no formal process need to enforce this. Through self-organization a team will adjust its size autonomously until optimal performance is reached. This will even happen across multiple teams working together. There is no external body who knows how to organize work better than the people actually undertaking the work.

In his groundbreaking book 'Drive' Daniel Pink elaborates on the scientific evidence of what motivates people. He describes how such 'self-directiveness', the ability for people to direct their own work, is one of three crucial motivators in cognitive, creative work (Pink, 2009). *'Mastery' and 'Purpose' complement it. Together they make what Pink identifies as the third drive, the model for human motivation that*

*follows the first drive of surviving and the second drive of industrial-like
Taylorist schemes implementing 'carrot and stick' rewards.*

However, autonomy and self-organization don't resolve all problems.
Some problems go beyond the self-organization of the Development
Team. Scrum calls those 'impediments'.

The general definition of an impediment is an *'obstruction; hindrance;
obstacle'*. An impediment in Scrum is a factor that blocks the
(Development) team in its creation of a valuable piece of software
in a Sprint, or that restricts the team in achieving its intrinsic level
of progress. It is the responsibility of the Scrum Master to remove
impediments.

The Scrum concept of 'impediments' however is not a replacement
for the traditional escalation procedures. An impediment is only an
impediment if it indeed surpasses the self-organizing capabilities of
the team, if it cannot be tackled within the self-organizing ecosystem.

Let's illustrate this with the example of a team conflict, a conflict
between team members.

A team might have problems in resolving an inner-team conflict
and call the conflict an impediment, expecting the Scrum Master
to remove it for them. Essentially they expect the Scrum Master to
resolve the conflict.

However, working as a team inevitably includes getting to know
each other, finding ways of building software together, exploring
different ways to collaborate, finding consensus over differing ideas,
outgrowing the desire for personal heroism. In her book, 'Coaching
Agile Teams' (Adkins, 2010), Lyssa Adkins elaborates on 'constructive

disagreement' as a necessity for teams[4]. This lowest level of conflict connects with the 'built-in instability' observed and described by Takeuchi and Nonaka as the fertile ground for successful complex product development (Takeuchi and Nonaka, 1986). It is a natural part of the freedom given to a group of people to jointly discover the best ways to move forward, in the absence of an external authority that prescribes the solution.

Conflicts are a natural part of working with people, of working as a team. It's part of self-organization, part of aiming at high performance. If a team raises it with the Scrum Master, we should wonder what the real problem is. Is it the Scrum Master's role to resolve the conflict? Or would that be an undesired intervention in the self-organizing ecosystem, undermining future honesty, learning and self-improvement?

How can the Scrum Master facilitate self-organization? Is it by offering teams an excuse, an external decision to hide behind? A Scrum Master, as the promoter of Scrum and self-organization, should consider how to help a team work out their problems themselves and offer any tools, trainings and insights on how best to do this.

### 2.6.3 Empirical process control
Software development is a complex activity in itself and it serves to build complex products in complex circumstances.

One perspective on the degree of 'complexity' relates to the number of parameters, variables and events that influence an activity and its course. In software development some of the more commonly known parameters are requirements, skills, experience, people, teams, technology, technical integrations, market conditions, regulations and dependencies.

However, it is not only the number of known parameters that's important, but also the knowledge of these parameters, the *available* knowledge as well as the *required* knowledge. What is the level of detail required to comprehend a variable as well as the future behavior of the variable? Even if a parameter is known, the level of detail may be too deep to be able to manage and control it. And then, of course, the behavior of the parameter is still not necessarily predictable. A variable may behave completely differently to what is expected.

'Complexity' is also dependent on the nature of the activity itself. The exact and detailed outcomes of software development are hard to describe and predict before or at the beginning of the actual development. The steps, tasks and activities that combine to make the actual software development work aren't predictable with any degree of high precision. People perform them, and the involvement of people is dependent on many circumstances. And then there's also working with technology itself, where technology evolves constantly and is dependent on the particularity of the organization's environment.

The steps, tasks and activities of software development aren't predictable to any degree of precision because they are not repeatable. Every 'product' being built is unique, new technologies emerge, new interfaces need to be built, new plug-ins are used, new integrations need to be set up, new insights and techniques for programming are discovered daily.

The degree of dynamism of a problem or activity requires the right process to be in place in order to have control over the activity:

■ *Open loop system:* All of the variables are gathered upfront because they need to be presented to the system, where in a single run a number of steps are performed resulting in a predicted outcome (figure 2.9). In order to have predictability of the elapsed time, this type of process control assumes a high degree of predictability of the variables that influence the process as well as of the process activities themselves.

To gain control over large or complex problems, in an open loop system, subsystems are created where each subsystem is an open loop system. Each subsystem is presented with the output of the previous subsystem. In situations of increased turbulence and frequent change, deviations and variances will accumulate across the various subsystems, far beyond acceptable levels and will only be detected at the end of the final subsystem.

Figure 2.9 Open loop system

Predictive plans are expressions of the industrial paradigm and implementations of open loop thinking. But predictive plans can only include known variables, and their *expected* behavior. Predictive plans create the illusion that the behavior of the known variables is precisely understood and that other variables are non-existent. Predictive plans invite lengthy upfront consideration of all elements that should be part of the plan, and attempt to foresee the unforeseeable. In order to control non-predicted variables or unexpected behavior weighty procedures are required to check, maintain and update the predictive plan.

■ *Closed loop system:* The actual outcome of the system is regularly compared to the desired outcome, in order to eliminate or gradually diminish any undesired variances (figure 2.10). Not all variables and parameters need to be known precisely and in detail upfront, as the process applies self-correction and takes into account new or changing parameters. This technique of regular inspections requires and creates transparency. The real situation is inspected, and exposed, so that the most appropriate adaptations can be undertaken to close the gap between the effective and the expected outputs. The people performing the inspections, the inspectors, need clear and agreed standards in order to carry out their inspections. Hence the need for transparency of the process and all its variables for all players involved.

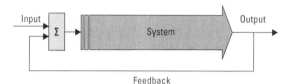

Figure 2.10 Closed loop system

Scrum acknowledges that the complexity of software development requires the right process, i.e. closed loop feedback. Scrum replaces the open loops of traditional processes with the *empiricism* of closed loop systems. Scrum implements regular inspection and adaptation opportunities at which the players can learn from an inspection, gather feedback over the output and improve. Scrum brings reality-based control over software development.

Scrum implements two specific closed-loop feedback cycles. A Sprint forms an 'inspect and adapt' cycle that wraps the 24-hours 'inspect and adapt' of the Daily Scrum:

■ *The Daily Scrum:* The Development Team inspects its progress, and estimates and plans its tasks within the container of the Sprint. *All of these elements were initially laid out in the Sprint Planning.* They use the Sprint Backlog, the Sprint Goal and a progress trend to consider the remaining effort. It assures they don't get out of sync with each other in the team and with the Sprint Goal for more than 24 hours.

- *The Sprint:* A Sprint is a cycle that starts with forecasting the work and ends with an inspection of what was actually built, the product Increment, including how it was built, the process, the team interactions and the technology.

The events of Scrum set the frequency of the inspection and adaptation, where the artifacts contain the information to be inspected and adapted (figure 2.11):

| Event | Inspection | Adaptation |
|---|---|---|
| Sprint Planning | • Product Backlog<br>• (Commitment Retrospective)<br>• (Definition of Done) | • Sprint Goal<br>• Sprint Backlog<br>• Forecast |
| Daily Scrum | • Sprint Progress<br>• (Sprint Goal) | • Sprint Backlog<br>• Daily Plan |
| Sprint Review | • Product Increment<br>• Product Backlog<br>• (Release Progress) | • Product Backlog |
| Sprint Retrospective | • Team & collaboration<br>• Technology & engineering<br>• Definition of Done | • Actionable improvements |

Figure 2.11 Scrum's Empiricism

These are the formal events that Scrum foresees as opportunities to inspect and adapt to the actual situation, so that the art of empiricism is performed no later than at the time of these events. This should not impede team members from improving and discussing improvements and progress whenever required. In a world of high dynamism that leads to using the Scrum framework it would be very strange if teams did not capitalize on new information and insights that improve their development life as soon as possible.

# ■ 2.7   THE SCRUM VALUES

Scrum, as has been demonstrated, is a framework of rules, roles and principles that helps people and organizations to develop a working process that is specific and appropriate to their time and context. Scrum implements empiricism as this is the most optimal process to enable control over complexity.

The framework of Scrum is based upon some core values (Schwaber & Beedle, 2001). Although these values were not invented as a part of Scrum, and are not exclusive to Scrum, they do give direction to the work, behavior and actions in Scrum (figure 2.12).

In a Scrum context the decisions we take, the steps we take, the way we play the game, the practices we add and the activities we surround Scrum with, should all re-enforce these values, not diminish or undermine them.

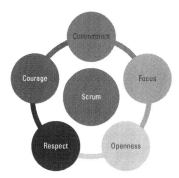

Figure 2.12 The Scrum values

### 2.7.1 Commitment

A general definition of 'commitment' is "*the state or quality of being dedicated to a cause, activity, etc.* It can be illustrated by a team's trainer stating "*I could not fault my players for commitment*".

This describes exactly how it was originally intended to be used in Scrum. Commitment is about dedication and applies to the actions and the intensity of the effort. It is not about the final result.

Yet, there was a widely spread misinterpretation of the word commitment in a Scrum context. This originates mainly from the past expectation of the Scrum framework that said teams should 'commit' to the Sprint. Through the lens of the old, industrial paradigm this was wrongly translated into an expectation that all scope selected at the Sprint Planning would be completed by the Sprint Review, *no matter*. 'Commitment' was wrongly converted into a hard-coded contract.

In the complex, creative and highly unpredictable world of software development, a promise of exact scope against time and budget is not possible. Too many variables influencing the outcome are unknown or may show unpredictable behavior.

To better reflect the original intent and connect more effectively to empiricism, 'commitment' in the context of scope for a Sprint was replaced with 'forecast'.

However, commitment still is and remains a core value of Scrum:

The players commit to the team. Commit to quality. Commit to collaborate. Commit to learn. Commit to do the best they can, every day again. Commit to the Sprint Goal. Commit to act as a professional. Commit to self-organize. Commit to excellence. Commit to the Agile principles. Commit to create working software. Commit to look for improvements. Commit to the definition of done. Commit to the Scrum framework. Commit to focus on value. Commit to finish work. Commit to inspect and adapt. Commit to transparency. Commit to challenge the status-quo.

### 2.7.2 Focus

The balanced but distinct roles of Scrum enable all players to focus on their expertise.

The time-boxing of Scrum encourages the players to focus on what's most important *now* without being bothered by considerations of what might stand a chance of becoming important at some point in the future. They focus on what they know *now*. YAGNI ('You Ain't Gonna Need It'), a principle from eXtreme Programming that effectively captures the focus of Agile, helps in retaining that focus. They focus on what's imminent as the future is highly uncertain and the players want to learn from the present in order to gain experience for future work. They focus on the work needed to get things done. They focus on the simplest thing that might possibly work.

The Sprint Goal gives focus to a period of 30 days, or less. Within that period, the Daily Scrum helps people collaboratively focus on the daily work.

### 2.7.3 Openness

The empiricism of Scrum requires transparency, openness, and honesty. The player-inspectors want to check on the current situation in order to make sensible adaptations. The players are open about their work, progress, learning and problems. But they are also open for people, and working with people; acknowledging people to be people, and not 'resources', robots or replaceable pieces of machinery.

The players are open to collaborate across disciplines, skills and job descriptions. They are open to collaborate with stakeholders and the wider environment. Open in sharing feedback and learning from one another.

They are open for change as the organization and the world in which they operate change; unpredictably, unexpectedly and constantly.

### 2.7.4  Respect

The broad Scrum ecosystem shows respect for people, their experience and their personal background. The players respect diversity. They respect different opinions. They respect each other's skills, expertise and insights.

They respect the wider environment by not behaving as an isolated island in the world. They respect the fact that customers change their mind. They show respect for the sponsors by not building features that will never be used and that increase the cost of the software. They show respect by not wasting money on things that are not valuable, not appreciated or might never be implemented or used anyhow. They show respect for users by fixing their problems.

All players respect the Scrum framework. They respect the accountabilities of the Scrum roles.

### 2.7.5  Courage

The players show courage in not building stuff that nobody wants. Courage in admitting that requirements will never be perfect and that no plan can capture reality and complexity.

They show the courage to consider change as a source of inspiration and innovation. Courage to not deliver incomplete software. Courage in sharing all possible information that might help the team and the organization. Courage in admitting that nobody is perfect. Courage to change direction. Courage to share risks and benefits. Courage to let go of the feint certainties of the past.

The players show courage in promoting Scrum and empiricism to deal with complexity.

They show courage to support the Scrum Values. The courage to take a decision and make progress, not grind, and even more courage to change that decision.

### Notes

[1] Object-Oriented Programming, Systems, Languages & Applications.

[2] 31% indicated not to be following any methodology. 21% indicated they were doing iterative development.

[3] Find an excerpt of the referred book at http://alistair.cockburn.us/Information+radiator.

[4] Find an excerpt of this part of the referred book at http://agile.dzone.com/articles/agile-managing-conflict.

Scrum – A Pocket Guide

# 3 Tactics for a purpose

Scrum has been around for more than 20 years. Over these years the framework has gradually evolved via small functional updates. The basic elements are still the same, as are the principles and rules that bind them together. But the mandatory prescriptions of Scrum grow... lighter, as the evolution of the Scrum Guide (Schwaber & Sutherland, 2013) shows.

The focus of the framework is still changing toward describing 'what' is expected, i.e. the purpose of the rules, from an understanding of the 'why' of the rules, as opposed to instructing 'how' to exactly apply the rules.

The previous chapter describes the rules to playing the game of Scrum. But the rules of the Scrum framework leave room for different *tactics* to play the game, tactics that are at any time right-size and can be fitted to context and circumstances. It's as in all games and sports, every team plays by the same set of rules, yet some teams are more successful than others. Success depends on many factors, and not all are equally controllable by the teams themselves, but success is certainly influenced by the tactics chosen to play the game.

It is like selecting good practices from a collection of such good practices and turning them into best practices by applying and tuning them to a specific context. Scrum can be called a 'process', but it's a *servant* process, not a *commanding* process. Scrum does not say what practice to do, or not to do. Scrum helps discover whether it works, but leaves it to the players to keep on doing it, or changing it.

There are many tactics to use within Scrum. Good tactics serve the purpose of Scrum. Good tactics re-enforce the Scrum values, rather than undercut them.

Let's take a closer look at some examples to clarify the difference between tactics and rules:

## ■ 3.1 VISUALIZING PROGRESS

A good illustration of an evolution of the Scrum framework towards more lightness is the elimination of burn-down charts as mandatory.

Looking at the rules of Scrum, including the need for transparency, which is crucial to the process of inspection and adaptation, and self-organization, it is clear 'why' it is important to visualize progress. Self-correction is difficult to achieve without it.

The former obligation, however, to use burn-down charts for it (the 'how') has been removed. The form or format of the visualization is no longer prescribed. It is replaced by the mere, but explicit, expectation that progress on the mandatory Scrum artifacts of Product Backlog and Sprint Backlog is visualized (the 'what').

Burn-down charts are still a great way to play the game and are suitable in many situations. Yet, they have been turned into a non-mandatory, good practice.

Yes, it's Scrum if the Backlogs exist and a visualization of their progress is available, accessible and clear. But there are multiple good practices for that visualization. It may be a burn-down chart with open effort. It may be a Cumulative Flow Diagram. It may be as simple as a Scrum board. For the progress on Product Backlog it may also be a burn-up chart in value.

## ■ 3.2   THE DAILY SCRUM QUESTIONS

Scrum suggests that in the Daily Scrum meeting every player of the team answers three questions with regards to the progress of the team towards its Sprint Goal (*Done? Planned? Impediments?*).

But even if the players answer the questions, they can still limit it to a personal status update. They might use the walls or the Scrum Board for presentation purposes. They might just make sure that they simply answer the three questions. This is because of the inability to look beyond the prescription of Scrum that tells them to answer the question. The rules are formally followed without understanding the 'why'.

Is the team merely seeing Scrum as a methodology? Or is the team using Scrum as a framework for discovery and collaboration? It doesn't help much whether they formally answer the three questions or not if they don't actually talk to each other. It doesn't help much if they don't reveal the information to optimize their shared work plan for the next 24 hours against the Sprint Goal. Maybe they use the meeting only as a reporting obligation, as a mental remainder of the industrial paradigm. Maybe they feel pressured to make sure all their micro-tasks are logged, and cover themselves against possible blame.

But in doing so, they miss the opportunity to gain insight in the real situation, to inspect it and to adapt it.

The goal of the Daily Scrum is to share information, and to re-plan the Development Team's collective work so that they progress in the best possible way towards the Sprint Goal. That should be the background from which the three questions are addressed, not blindly to go through the three questions from a 'best practice' viewpoint.

*Did you know that a Daily Scrum is not necessarily a Daily Stand-up?*

The Daily Stand-up is the practice described in eXtreme Programming (Beck, 2000) that serves the same purpose as the Daily Scrum in Scrum. But eXtreme Programming tells participants to do it while standing up.

Scrum has no obligation to do it standing up. However, it is a good tactic, especially to keep the time-box within 15 minutes.

## ■ 3.3 PRODUCT BACKLOG REFINEMENT

Refinement of the Product Backlog is an on-going activity during a Sprint in which the Development Team and the Product Owner look at the Product Backlog currently ordered for one of the next Sprints. There is a growing certainty that the items are actually going to be implemented as the timing gets closer.

As items come closer in time, teams might want to unveil dependencies, understand better what is expected from the work, decide on a shared approach for its development or help a Product Owner understand the development impact at a functional level. Collaborative refinement of Product Backlog, and the additional knowledge that emerges from the refinement conversation, increases the chances that the work might actually, or more easily, be pulled into a Sprint when it is presented at Sprint Planning.

Product Backlog refinement is not an official, time-boxed Scrum event. The ambition of Scrum is to remain simple, yet sufficient. The ambition of Scrum is to help people and teams discover additional practices that may or may not be appropriate in their specific context. Product Backlog refinement is an activity that many teams undertake to smoothen their Sprints, and limit turbulence in the first days of a Sprint. A typical feature of Product Backlog refinement activities is that estimates of effort or cost get set, or are revised. Other teams may be much further down their Agile path, need less precision at Sprint Planning or have a relationship with the Product Owner that's less about accuracy. They cope without it, or do it less formally, do it without explicitly naming or consciously planning this activity. They would perceive it as optional or even as an overhead if it was a mandatory event instructed by the Scrum framework.

Product Backlog refinement is a great activity within a Sprint, a good tactic to collaboratively manage Product Backlog. Some can do without however.

## ■ 3.4   USER STORIES

In eXtreme Programming (Beck, 2000) requirements are captured in 'User Stories'. User Stories are written on index cards, and describe functional expectations from a user's perspective. Bill Wake, an early practitioner of eXtreme Programming, suggested the 'INVEST' acronym as a simple way to remember and assess whether or not a User Story is well formed: Independent, Negotiable, Valuable, Estimable, Sized appropriately, Testable. (For details see http://xp123. com/articles/invest-in-good-stories-and-smart-tasks/.)

User Stories typically describe a feature, the 'Story', from the perspective of the 'User'. The advantage of taking the user's perspective to describe the system or application requirement is the focus on the value of the work for that user.

Index cards are easy to move around on, or remove from, a planning board, as an information radiator. Another advantage of using physical index cards for a story is the limited space for textual descriptions and details. It ensures that it is incomplete by design and in this way makes sure that conversation takes place as a result of a story. As a User Story comes closer in time, and the chances grow that it will get implemented, it necessarily requires discussion to discover additional details. More information may be added to the card, and some of this may be expressed as acceptance criteria for the User Story. Such acceptance criteria are typically written on the back of the card.

A Product Backlog in Scrum serves to provide transparency to *all* work that a Scrum Team needs to do. This comprises more than just functional requirements. Although the User Story format may be used for other types of requirements, there is no natural fit. And it tends to lay the focus on the syntax, away from the information that's to be conveyed.

There is no obligation, from Scrum, to use the User Story format for Product Backlog items. It risks forgetting other important work that needs to be undertaken, or it might force teams to spend more time and energy on using the 'right' format, thus creating waste. However, for functional items on the Product Backlog, User Stories can be very good, a great tactic.

## ■ 3.5   PLANNING POKER

Planning Poker is an estimation technique invented by James
Grenning during an eXtreme Programming project where he suffered
from having to spend too much time on producing estimates.

In Planning Poker a team has a discussion about a requirement,
after which every team member decides on an estimate for the
requirement by picking a value from a set of poker cards. Poker
cards typically use an exponential scale like the Fibonacci sequence
(1, 2, 3, 5, 8, 13, 21, 34, ...). All team members keep their chosen value
to themselves until everybody has done so. They then reveal their
estimate at the same time, after which they continue the conversation
over possible differences. This cycle is repeated until agreement and
a joint understanding of the requirements are reached. Estimates
are generally relative to each other and are expressed in an abstract
unit, like (Story) points or even gummy bears as in early eXtreme
Programming projects.

In Scrum, estimates on Product Backlog items are the ultimate
responsibility of the Development Team. As part of transparency and
collaboration, it is required to have honest and unbiased estimates
from the complete Development Team.

Although not mandatory, Planning Poker is a good tactic for that
principle. But don't forget that the ultimate intention is to invoke an
honest discussion about the estimates, because this results in a good
understanding of the work attached to implementing the discussed
item.

## ■ 3.6   SPRINT LENGTH

Scrum only determines the maximum length of a Sprint, i.e. no more
than four weeks (or 30 days, or a calendar month). This maximum

length ensures that nobody is deprived of the right to inspect a piece of working software at least every 30 days and to adapt the future plans. Also the team does not have to be locked away in a container for too long, which risks them losing a grip on the changing world.

Sprint length holds a balance between focus and opportunistic adaptiveness. The balance should be business driven.

In an empirical process like Scrum, control objectives are presented to a system and, via closed-loop feedback, results are regularly inspected against these objectives in order to adapt materials, tasks and processes. Skilled inspectors, the roles foreseen by Scrum, carry out inspections at an appropriate frequency, so the focus and time required to create valuable output are balanced against the risk of allowing too much variance in the created output.

In addition to transparency, frequency is an important factor in empiricism. The Scrum events determine the frequency of the inspections and adaptations in Scrum, with the Sprint being a container event, the outer feedback loop.

There is a tendency to move to shorter Sprints. Although not a formal obligation, one week Sprints seem like an acceptable minimum.

Let's have a look at this by presuming that a team does one-day Sprints. All Scrum events, as opportunities to inspect and adapt, take place in the same day, and are organized at a high frequency. There is a significant danger that a Scrum Team will focus merely on its daily work and progress. They will take no time to inspect and adapt the overall process, or probe for ways to improve quality or connect to an overarching goal and objectives. They will just try to get more product out the door, every day.

Sprint length also determines the frequency at which the Product Owner and the Development Team consult with stakeholders over a working version of the product. This reveals important information and it helps the Product Owner to make the decision on a release of the product Increment. In the case of one-day Sprints, stakeholder buy-in will be more difficult to achieve, let alone capture and adapt to enterprise, market and strategic changes.

Sprint length should take into account the risk of losing a business opportunity because Sprints are too long. If your business is indeed so volatile that you risk losing opportunities by spending more than one day in the container of a Sprint, please do one day Sprints and release daily. But be careful of burning the inspection mechanisms with such high frequency and organize work that is sustainable indefinitely.

Consider your Sprint length as a tactic to play Scrum. See how it works and adapt accordingly, bearing in mind stability, heartbeat and sustainable pace.

## 3.7 SCALING SCRUM

We have described the basic rules to play the game of Scrum. The rules remain consistent and are independent of the scale at which Scrum is organized.

Scrum promotes simplicity. Scrum promotes clear accountability and peer collaboration to deal with unpredictability and formulate answers to complex problems.

Simplicity, bottom-up accountability and collaboration were not at the core of many enterprises when scaling their organizations and their work. The main challenge in scaling Scrum lies not in fitting Scrum into the existing structures, but to revise the existing structures via a bottom-up understanding, implementation and growth of Scrum, while keeping the base rules of the game intact and respecting them.

There are some tactics that allow Scrum to be played on a larger scale, depending on the context.

### 3.7.1 Serial Scrum

The simplest situation for undertaking product development with Scrum is to have Product Backlog capturing the desirements for the product, and having one Scrum Team implementing the Product Backlog in time-boxed Sprints (figure 3.1).

The Development Team has all the skills to turn several Product Backlog items into a shippable product Increment per Sprint, guided therein by the definition of done. The Development Team manages its work autonomously via Sprint Backlog and has a daily inspection to safeguard direction and alignment via the Daily Scrum. The Product Owner provides right-time functional and business clarifications. The Scrum Master coaches, facilitates and serves the team and the organization.

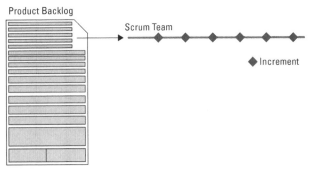

Figure 3.1  A serial Scrum implementation

The biggest challenge lies in having all development skills collaborating as one team. But if that problem is overcome, the Sprint Review is fully transparent, an important prerequisite to make the empirical approach of Scrum work. The team uses the Sprint Retrospective to improve itself.

### 3.7.2 Multiple Scrum Teams
For larger products or faster results, the need to create and release a product with multiple Scrum Teams may surface (figure 3.2).

The multiple Scrum Teams build one product, i.e. work on the same Product Backlog. Each Scrum Team has a Product Owner, Development Team and Scrum Master. Each Scrum Teams selects Product Backlog items to create a forecast, and designs a Sprint Backlog for that forecast. Each Development Team self-inspects via a Daily Scrum meeting.

The need for a transparent 'inspection' at the Sprint Review remains. Transparency enables the Product Owner to decide on releasing the Increment of the product to the users. The Increment should still have no undone, hidden work left, and should technically be releasable. However, the multiple Scrum Teams are jointly building the same product. Only an inspection of an *integrated* Increment assures the Product Owner, and the stakeholders, of complete transparency.

The multiple Scrum Teams self-organize, within the boundaries of the Scrum rules and principles. When working with multiple Scrum Teams, i.e. several teams creating and sustaining the same product, the teams will self-organize against the expectation of creating an integrated Increment in every Sprint.

On top of the Daily Scrum per team, the teams need regular communication across the multiple Scrum Teams to align their work plans within the Sprint against the objective of creating an integrated Increment. The Scrum Teams scale the principle of a Daily Scrum to a cross-team level and do *Scrum-of-Scrums* meetings.

The most appropriate representatives of the Development Teams gather regularly to exchange development information, so that each Scrum Team can optimally re-plan and adjust its Sprint Backlog. As a result, the multiple Scrum Teams optimize their joint progress towards an integrated Increment of product by the end of each Sprint. The usable Increment can be released upon the assessment by the Product Owner of whether it has the right level of usefulness.

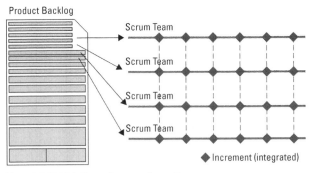

Figure 3.2  Multiple Scrum Teams scaling pattern

The multiple Scrum Teams work against the same quality criteria for the product as expressed in the definition of done. The multiple Scrum Teams will most likely work on the same Sprint length in order to simplify planning and integration. Additional work will be foreseen in their Sprint Backlogs to keep their work integrated and healthy.

### 3.7.3 Multiple products

At a portfolio or program level, the planning and implementation of several products may need to be aligned and synchronized. For each product a Product Backlog exists with one Scrum Team or multiple Scrum Teams to create and sustain it (figure 3.3).

From the accountabilities of Scrum it is clear that alignment and synchronization are undertaken on the Product Backlogs by the Product Owners. Product Backlogs are ordered on an additional program or portfolio factor. The Product Owners, thereby assisted and facilitated by the organization, incrementally manage their Product Backlogs on the basis of shared information and shared progress.

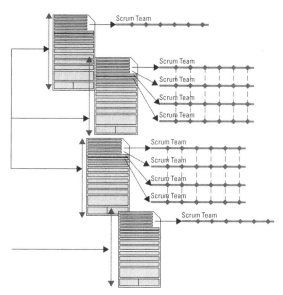

Figure 3.3 Scrum scaling pattern to handle multiple products

Many more scaling problems, and therefore scenarios, exist. There is not one silver bullet solution. Scrum promotes bottom-up thinking with top-down support to discover and emerge what works best for you, your organization and your context (Schwaber & Sutherland, 2012).

# 4 The future state of Scrum

## ■ 4.1 YES, WE DO SCRUM. AND...

Scrum emerged in the 1990's from the work and discovery of Ken Schwaber and Jeff Sutherland. They critically analyzed practices which at that time were considered as common in software development, their own professional experience, successful product development techniques (Takeuchi & Nonaka, 1986) and process control theory. The sum of their findings became Scrum (Schwaber, 1995). In the years that have passed since the publication of the 'Manifesto for Agile Software Development' in 2001, Scrum became the most applied framework worldwide for Agile software development.

Yet, Scrum has remained a light and simple way to organize software development based upon the Agile principles and ideas. In my opinion, the low-prescriptive nature of Scrum is the foundation for its success. Scrum, as an organizational framework, can wrap existing product development practices or render some of these existing practices superfluous. Scrum is likely to reveal the need for new practices. The benefits of Scrum will be greater when complemented by improved or revised engineering, product management, people and organizational practices. But the core is stable.

Over the first two decades of its existence, organizations have primarily used Scrum to add predictability to the IT and technology aspects of software development. For many IT people worldwide, the Scrum framework has become a proven solution. Despite the great results, like Agile overtaking waterfall and the gorilla position of Scrum, there is room for improvement. There is a need to take it further.

Challenging the status quo of the industrial paradigm has improved continuous learning in dealing with many *technological* uncertainties in the ICT domain. And in many organizations the understanding has been restored that software development is a creative and complex activity. But that focus is on 'how' software is built. It is time to elaborate on the achieved results and take Scrum adoption to the next level.

There is a myriad of possibilities to play and complement Scrum, and the results and performance of Scrum are influenced by many factors. The co-location of people influences it. The energy, dedication and joy of the people-players influence it. The level of self-organization influences it. The fact whether people have to multi-task influences it. The availability of engineering and testing automation, tools, platforms and practices influences it.

A crucial aspect is the cross-functional thinking that goes beyond the walls of the IT department through the enterprise. Remember that Agile software development is driven by business opportunities. From having implemented Scrum for the 'how' of product development, adding more focus now to 'what' needs to be built is crucial. That shift will help organizations discover the power of the possible product, reduce the amount of product built, instead of merely optimizing the way that the product is being developed (see section 4.2).

There is a myriad of techniques and practices to play Scrum and to add
to Scrum. But more than process and techniques, moving from the
old, industrial paradigm to the new Agile paradigm is about culture
and behavior. The common bottom-up enthusiasm that arises from
doing Scrum is unlikely to be sufficient for such transformation.
For a lasting effect the common bottom-up enthusiasm needs to be
supported and facilitated by upstream adoption (see section 4.3).

## ■ 4.2  THE POWER OF THE POSSIBLE PRODUCT

The development of software products can be much improved if
we deal better with *what* software is being built; the requirements,
features and functions.

In turbulent enterprise, business and market circumstances, the
certainty and stability of software requirements is low. Improved and
active collaboration with business owners and product managers is a
natural next step in optimizing software product development. Only
the people accountable for the business value of the software products
can help to overcome the unavoidable absence of full agreement over
features and requirements. And more than ever these product people
do need the flexibility to capitalize on unforeseen opportunities in
order to build the best possible product at the right time.

The Scrum framework allows people to give up on trying to predict
the unpredictable, as it deals with answers, solutions and competing
ideas that emerge while building. Scrum renders the question of
whether issues were thought of upfront as irrelevant. Requirements
as the input for software development system are no longer expected
to be complete, final and exhaustive. Scrum helps by accepting – and
embracing – the fact that the final agreement on the 'what' of the
software product only gets resolved while creating it. Scrum helps
by validating internal decisions frequently against the usage of the

software product in the marketplace. Scrum opens the door for, and promotes, frequent functional releases as the best way to progress, since they build in regular feedback from customers and do not merely accumulate assumptions from customer representatives via sequential open loop systems. Real user feedback can be easily incorporated as emerging requirements when connection to the marketplace is tight.

In Scrum, the Product Owner is the only one telling the Development Team what to build (next). The Product Owner consolidates the work from the Development Team into a next release or version of the product for the marketplace. The mandate of the Product Owner influences the level of improvement and agility an organization achieves with Scrum. On top of the mandate, a Scrum Product Owner needs a close connection to all related product management domains: marketing, communication, legal, research, finance, etc.

It is equally essential to promote multi-disciplined collaboration across organizational walls in product management. The capability to adapt these parts of an organization leverages the use of Scrum for *enterprise* agility. In a globalizing world of internal and external unpredictability, adopting a mindset of empiricism and adaptiveness is beneficial to entire organizations.

The utilization of Scrum is not about renaming or slightly reworking old techniques, techniques that are rooted in the industrial paradigm. Product people are not being asked to hand over a list of User Stories as a replacement for the old requirements documents. Nor does it suffice for analysts to act as proxies for the product people if they lack a mandate, stakeholder backing, budget responsibility and real user accountability.

Scrum Sprints are the core of overall business agility in generating a continuous flow of improvements, learnings and various other sources of value. In the end, an enterprise and its markets become a self-balancing continuum, with players contributing across barriers, domains, skills and functions. Organizations can discover, experiment and deliver opportunities from an end-to-end perspective in the fastest possible way.

## ▪ 4.3    THE UPSTREAM ADOPTION OF SCRUM

When adopting Scrum, the broader organization is impacted. Issues that go beyond the Scrum Teams will come up and need to be taken care of in order to gain the full benefit of Scrum, to better facilitate the Scrum Teams and thereby improve product development. Organizational opportunities and improvement areas are discovered through the application of Scrum.

Organizations wanting to use Scrum to make progress on their path to agility should be aware that this will not be achieved by implementing Scrum just for the sake of it. Scrum has the potential of being a *tool* to be Agile at an organizational, enterprise level. Scrum is not designed to be just a new IT process, but rather as a framework of rules, roles and events to enable organizations to capitalize on the unforeseeable. Scrum enables fast adaptation to follow the market and the competition (again).

A vast majority of organizations unfortunately act as if they still reside in the land of *Mediocristan*. The characteristics for that 'state' of society, as described by Nassim Nicholas Taleb in his sublime book 'The Black Swan' (Taleb, 2007), are that success has a direct relationship to the hours or effort spent on non-scalable, repetitive work. Taleb describes how Mediocristan has become an illusion of the past, and has been replaced by *Extremistan*, where success depends on the 'production' of ideas and the elaboration of the unpredicted singularity. Scrum has what it takes to beam up the inhabitants of Mediocristan to Extremistan so they become at least 'a' player in Extremistan, or even a leader, a giant. Scrum can be the engine for adapting so fast that it's up to your competitors to respond to the change you cause. Leading the game comes within reach, to outnumber the rest of the population, to be the giant.

But it starts with accepting, if not embracing, that we do live in a market state of Extremistan. It starts with accepting that our organizations must change not to fade. The fundamentals on which they are constructed have been invalidated. *Our iceberg is melting*, is the metaphor in the tale of Holger Rathgeber and renowned change expert John P. Kotter (Kotter & Rathgeber, 2006). It is the cause of a lack of upstream adoption for Scrum and it limits the benefits from the game of Scrum, and undermines your future leadership, and even survival.

In larger organizations, Scrum Teams and their Scrum Masters have limited or no control over the formal delivery and release obligations of software products. Often teams have to operate on the basis of compliancy expectations and ceremonial rules that have been designed as part of the industrial paradigm. They are being maintained beyond the actual experiences of building products and lack of success. In many cases they have grown out of step with the rapid evolutions that are so typical for today's markets, external circumstances and internal organizational evolutions.

Nevertheless, the experience of Scrum in a vast majority of these cases is excellent, and lives up to a sense of common sense. The inhabitants of the house of Scrum appreciate Scrum because it thrives on and creates much enthusiasm. No surprise that this is exactly why *downstream adoption* is generally huge.

One would expect that great results, good figures and increased productivity lead to upstream success. Experience however contradicts this expectation.

Your organization deserves active and explicit upstream support and promotion of Scrum. Think about operational IT management, sales divisions, delivery managers, product departments and hierarchical CxO management.

It takes a sense of urgency, and the acceptance that there *is* indeed urgency. It starts by accepting the confrontational truth that no comfort, certainty and control will come from predictions. Comfort comes from reality, from proven experience and empirical data instead of static and gamed information. The traditional formalism has not resulted in improved execution. Requirements change, unexpected requirements appear, priorities shift.

Upstream adoption is a matter of management. Management is not useless just because Scrum has no explicit role for them. Scrum neither has prescriptions, artifacts, events or roles for lots of other interesting and useful tasks or activities within organizations.

The goal of a lasting Scrum transformation as a step on the path to Agility is to get managers involved in the game through a structured, iterative-incremental change program. Such a program thrives upon an urgency for improvement, thereby capitalizing on the bottom-up enthusiasm that exists over Scrum. Such a change program doesn't address organizational areas in a waterfall-way. A typical waterfall transition starts with an enterprise introducing Scrum and resolving the problem of cross-functional teams first. This often reveals a lack of engineering facilities and support, so that domain is tackled next. After addressing the engineering area, an enterprise might want to increase business involvement. And so on. Depending on the size of the enterprise, it can easily take one to three years per area.

A change program to transform an organization to Scrum addresses enterprise domains in parallel. Cross-functional change teams implement small steps in the domains in parallel while the overall effects of the steps are measured. The regular inspections of enterprise or product-level measurements form the base for an informed decision on the next steps and practices in the various domains. The vertical silo-like departments become dimmed. Barriers get removed. Communities emerge. Authority moves down the line. Accountability grows. Agility occurs. *But, remember Agility can't be planned.*

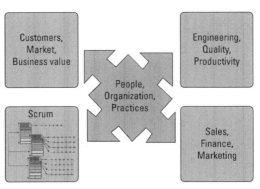

Figure 4.1 Enterprise Scrum transformation

The future state of Scrum will no longer be called 'Scrum'. What we now call Scrum will have become the norm, as the new paradigm for the software industry has taken over and organizations have re-invented themselves around it.

Scrum – A Pocket Guide

# Annex A: Scrum vocabulary and definitions

**Burn-down Chart**: a chart showing the evolution of remaining effort against time.

**Daily Scrum**: daily, time-boxed event to re-plan the development work during a Sprint. It serves for the Development Team to inspect the daily progress and update the Sprint backlog.

**Definition of done**: a list of expectations that software must live up to in order to be released into production.

**Development Team**: the role within a Scrum Team accountable for doing incremental development work, with the aim of creating a releasable Increment every Sprint.

**Emergence**: the process of the coming into existence or prominence of unforeseen facts or knowledge of a fact, a previously unknown fact, or knowledge of a fact becoming visible unexpectedly.

**Empiricism**: a process control type in which decisions are based on observation, experience and experimentation. Empiricism has three pillars: transparency, inspection and adaptation.

**Engineering standards**: a set of development and technology standards that a Development Team applies to create releasable Increments of software.

**Increment**: a piece of working software that adds to previously created Increments, and -as a whole – forms a software product.

**Product Backlog**: a list of the work to be done in order to create, maintain and sustain a software product.

**Product Backlog refinement**: the activity in a Sprint through which the Product Owner and the Development Team add granularity to Product Backlog.

**Product Owner**: the role within a Scrum Team accountable for incrementally managing and expressing business and functional expectations for a product.

**Scrum Master**: the role within a Scrum Team that is accountable for guiding, coaching, teaching and assisting a Scrum Team and its environments in the proper use of Scrum.

**Scrum Team**: a team consisting of a Product Owner, Development Team and Scrum Master.

**Scrum Values**: a set of fundamental values and qualities underpinning the Scrum framework.

**Sprint**: time-boxed event that serves as a container for the other Scrum events.

**Sprint Backlog**: an overview of the development work to realize the Sprint's goal.

**Sprint Goal**: a short phrase describing the purpose of a Sprint.

**Sprint Planning**: time-boxed event to start a Sprint. It serves for the Scrum Team to inspect the work that's most valuable to be done next and design that work into Sprint backlog.

**Sprint Retrospective**: time-boxed event to end a Sprint. It serves for the Scrum Team to inspect the past Sprint and update the process for the next Sprint.

**Sprint Review**: time-boxed event to end the development work of a Sprint. It serves for the Scrum Team and the stakeholders to inspect the Increment resulting from the Sprint, the impact of overall progress and update the Product backlog.

**Stakeholder**: a person external to the Scrum Team with a specific interest in and knowledge of a product that is required for incremental discovery.

**Velocity**: indication of the average amount of Product Backlog turned into an Increment of product during a Sprint by a Scrum Team.

# Annex B: References

Adkins, L. (2010). *Coaching Agile Teams, A Companion for ScrumMasters, Agile Coaches, and Project Managers in Transition.* Addison-Wesley.

Beck, K. (2000). *Extreme Programming Explained – Embrace Change.* Addison-Wesley.

Beck, K., Beedle, M., v. Bennekum, A., Cockburn, A., Cunningham, W., Fowler, M., Grenning, J., Highsmith, J., Hunt, A., Jeffries, R., Kern, J., Marick, B., Martin, R. C., Mellor, S., Schwaber, K., Sutherland, J., Thomas, D. (February 2001). *Manifesto for Agile Software Development.* http://agilemanifesto.org/

Benefield, G. (2008). *Rolling Out Agile at a Large Enterprise.* HICSS'41 (Hawaii International Conference on Software Systems).

Cockburn, A. (2002). *Agile Software Development.* Addison-Wesley.

Giudice, D. L. (November 2011). *Global Agile Software Application Development Online Survey.* Forrester Research.

Hammond, J., West, D. (October 2009). *Agile Application Lifecycle Management.* Forrester Research.

Kotter, J., Rathgeber, H. (2006). *Our Iceberg Is Melting, Changing and Succeeding Under Any Conditions.* MacMillan.

Larman, C. (2004). *Agile & Iterative Development, A Manager's Guide.* Addison-Wesley.

Larman, C., Vodde, B. (2009). *Lean Primer*. http://www.leanprimer.com

Moore, G. (1999). *Crossing the Chasm, Marketing and Selling Technology Products to Mainstream Customers (second edition)*. Wiley.

Pink, D. (2009). *Drive: The Surprising Truth About What Motivates Us*. Riverhead books.

Schwaber, K. (October 1995). SCRUM Software Development Process.

Schwaber, K., Beedle, M. (2001). *Agile Software Development with Scrum*. Prentice Hall.

Schwaber, K., Sutherland, J. (April 2012). *Software in 30 Days: How Agile Managers Beat the Odds, Delight Their Customers, and Leave Competitors in the Dust*. Wiley.

Schwaber, K., Sutherland, J. (July 2013). *The Scrum Guide*. Scrum.org.

Standish (2002). *Keynote on Feature Usage in a Typical System at XP2002 Congress* by Jim Johnson, Chairman of the Standish Group.

Standish (2011). *Chaos Manifesto (The Laws of Chaos and the Chaos 100 Best PM Practices)*. The Standish Group International.

Sutherland, J. (-) *Oopsla '95 – Business Object Design and Implementation Workshop*. http://www.jeffsutherland.org/oopsla/schwaber.html

Sutherland, J. (October 2011). *Takeuchi and Nonaka: The Roots of Scrum*. http://scrum.jeffsutherland.com/2011/10/takeuchi-and-nonaka-roots-of-scrum.html

Taleb, N. N. (2007). *The Black Swan – The Impact of the Highly Improbable*. Random House.

Takeuchi, H., Nonaka, I. (January-February 1986). *The New New Product Development Game*, Harvard Business Review.

Verheyen, G. (December 2011). *The Blending Philosophies of Lean and Agile*. Scrum.org (http://www.scrum.org/Community/Community-Publications)

Verheyen, G., Arooni, A. (December 2012). ING, *Capturing Agility via Scrum at a large Dutch bank*.

VersionOne (2011). *State of Agile Survey. 6th Annual.* VersionOne Inc.

VersionOne (2013). *7th Annul State of Agile Development Survey.* VersionOne Inc.

Wiefels, P. (2002). *The Chasm Companion. A Fieldbook to Crossing the Chasm and Inside the Tornado.* Wiley.

## About the author

 Gunther Verheyen (gunther.verheyen@ scrum.org) ventured into IT and software development after graduating as an Industrial Engineer in electronics in 1992. His Agile journey started with eXtreme Programming and Scrum in 2003/2004. Years of dedication followed, working with several teams and organizations doing Scrum in diverse circumstances. Utilizing the experience gained, Gunther gradually moved towards being the driving force behind some large-scale enterprise transformations.

Gunther currently works with Ken Schwaber and Scrum.org as Director of the 'Professional' series of Scrum.org. He shepherds the courseware and assessments for PSD, PSM, PSF, and PSPO. Gunther is also Professional Scrum trainer and contributor to Scrum.org's 'Agility Path' framework for increased Agility via enterprise transformations.

Gunther lives in Antwerp (Belgium) with his wife Natascha, and their sunshine children Ian, Jente and Nienke.

Find Gunther on Twitter as @ullizee or read more of his musings on Scrum on his personal blog, http://ullizee.wordpress.com.

### About Scrum.org

 Scrum.org leads the evolution and maturity of Scrum to improve the profession of software development, up to the level of the enterprise agility of organizations.

Scrum.org strives to provide all of the tools and resources needed by Scrum practitioners and experts in agility to deliver value using Scrum. In close collaboration with Jeff Sutherland, Scrum.org maintains the Scrum Guide in 30 languages. Scrum.org provides Scrum assessments to allow people to evaluate themselves and improve, hosts community forums and webcasts to foster discussion and knowledge transfer, and defines industry-leading Scrum training for practitioners at all levels. All these are part of the overall view of Scrum.org on enterprise agility as covered by the 'Agility Path' framework.

Scrum.org was founded in 2009 by Ken Schwaber, one of the creators of Scrum, along with Alex Armstrong, out of extreme dissatisfaction with the state of the art of software development.

Scrum.org is based in Boston, Massachusetts (USA).

"Scrum is free. Scrum's roles, artifacts, events, and rules are immutable and although implementing only parts of Scrum is possible, the result is not Scrum. Scrum exists only **in its entirety** and functions well as a container for other techniques, methodologies, and practices."

(Ken Schwaber, Jeff Sutherland, The Scrum Guide)